PRAYER
IN THE MORNING
A Book for Day's Beginning

❖ ❖

JIM COTTER

SHEFFIELD
CAIRNS PUBLICATIONS
1989

SEQUENCE

PREFACE

SIGNOR CHAPUYS, the Spanish Ambassador to the Court of King Henry VIII, is visiting the Lord Chancellor of England, Sir Thomas More, at his home in Chelsea. It is a scene from Robert Bolt's play, *A man for all seasons*. Chapuys has exchanged a Latin greeting with William Roper, More's son-in-law. He turns to More and says, "And how much longer shall we hear that holy language in these shores?" More replies, with dry wit, "'Tisn't holy, Your Excellency; just old."

The Christian Church has accumulated a mountain of prayers, psalms, scriptures, hymns, inspired (and not so inspired) writings, many of which have found their way into forms of corporate worship. At the heart of that prayer together is the Eucharist. At the heart of each individual's prayer are unique aspirations, confessions, thanksgivings, many of them having been influenced by that vast inheritance.

In between, used by local churches, religious communities, and some individuals, has been the tradition of the Daily Offices. Neither individualistic nor invariable, sometimes long, sometimes short, they have drawn on the inheritance. They are focused on psalms and intercession, praise and prayer. Shaped and altered over the centuries, they have been arranged in such a way as to respect and celebrate the weekly and seasonal rhythms of the year, and to bring before the praying mind and heart the rich variety of Christian truth and the many faces of the God of the Love.

However, as with possessions, the number of words has often increased and only with reluctance been pruned. As a result those who pray the Offices have found themselves faced with so many words to say that they have rattled through them rather than prayed through them. Of course it is *possible* to use many words and still to pray, but I suspect that this is so only for those in religious communities for whom the words have become a gentle murmur to keep the mind from wandering and thus distracting the praying heart.

The rest of us have to approach this kind of prayer differently. What is vital is to set aside a period of time to pray rather than to feel an obligation to say certain prescribed words. It is possible in five minutes to say the words suggested in this book for any one morning, but to say them with sufficient breathing space, sufficient silence for them to drop from mind to heart, need take only another five minutes, but would transform the reciting into praying.

Of equal importance is that the words themselves should ring true, and that they should be capable of being spoken aloud quietly with a certain modest relish, with sensitivity to their meanings and rhythms, and alert to a resonance that carries them into the praying heart and cherishes them there. Words may be no substitute for love, but they can be the bearers of love. They may in the end be straw, but they can be sacraments of God's presence. And even straw can be nourishing to spiritual donkeys.

So the reminder is apposite that what is old isn't necessarily holy. Not all that we have inherited is equally valuable. I suspect that one of the reasons for hurrying through words of prayer is that we do not have the courage to say that some of the inheritance no longer helps us to pray: what was once a glad duty, a way of love's renewal, turns into a sour obligation or embittered rejection. We hurry when we no longer value what we are doing and wish to get on with something else.

We need to be free to question and challenge, to prune the old and to compose new words for a new day. Indeed we should expect this if we believe that the Holy Spirit is still guiding us into the truth. For example, I doubt if more than a couple of dozen of the psalms are memorable as they stand. Parts of others, yes, odd lines here and there, but, in good Jewish fashion, there is much to continue to argue with, to work with and adapt, even to melt down and mint afresh.

Much of the material in this book is a result of that process. It can make no claims as poetry, but it is the attempt of one person to pray in the language of a heart that has been informed by words of our own day as well as those of former days. Together they may point the way to a more prayed response to the Mystery of Love, enabling that response to be more truthful.

But it would be a mistake to regard this book as sacrosanct in its turn. If some words jar, don't use them: discover something better. This is a quarry, a resource. If it fulfils its purpose, it will have alterations in it before long, according to the insights and approaches of individuals and groups using it. Indeed, this second edition is itself an example of that process at work.

Perhaps it will not be long before such a venture as this is produced on disk, with subscribers able to contribute to and to receive suggestions and amendments. A literacy of the elite produced a form of worship led by the few who could read; a literacy of the many has produced a form of worship where all can participate in the hymns and prayers produced by the few; a new technology will allow the many to contribute to the production itself.

Certainly the range of themes for prayer has not been exhausted in this book, either for our own personal pilgrimage or for our common life. For if this God of Love focused in Christ is the reality at the heart of the universe, there are implications for the shaping of our corporate life. This was true for the psalmists of Israel: so through our prayer God will revive in us the hunger and thirst for justice, for the Commonwealth, the Reign of God.

Because the material in this book has been mulled over for some years, I may not have acknowledged all the sources. Those I have been able to trace are listed but I apologize to any whose rights have been infringed. Any omissions will be rectified in future editions. And I am all too aware of a debt of gratitude to those of my contemporaries and of my ancestors of faith for their words of prayer, their shouts of joy, their cries, howls, and questions, their whispers and consolations. Once in a while we realize we are caught up in a great venture of faith and love, and words give way to silence and wonder.

JIM COTTER, May 1989

PREPARATION

PREPARATION

LET there be a settling and a becoming still.
Stretch, shake, and quieten the physical self.
Place both feet on the ground.
Sense the back straight but not stiff. . .

Make these mental suggestions
but do not physically alter position:
Let the neck be free. . .
Let the back widen and lengthen. . .
Let the head go forward and up. . .
Sense a plumb line from the top of the head
   to the base of the spine. . .

Become aware of your breathing. . .
Breathe out gently. . .
Let the air in. . .
Be aware of the rhythm. . .

Let there be no strain. . .
Let be. . .
Relax. . .

Let this prayer happen,
in tune with the breathing,
perhaps discovering appropriate physical movements:

I RECEIVE life from all around me:
To all around me I give life.

I breathe in Holy Spirit:
Holy Spirit breathes through me.

Spirit of Love, Companion and Lover,
open my heart that I may embrace you, my Beloved.

Spirit of Wisdom, Grandfather, Grandmother,
open my mind that I may know you, my Wise One.

Spirit of Creation, Thou That Shalt Be,
open my spirit that I may dream you, my Future.

Spirit of Yeshua, Incarnate Jesus,
open my flesh that I may embody you, my Saviour.

Spirit of the Living God,
open my whole being that I may dance your life this day.

Star of Dawn! Living Sun!
I greet you: Alleluia!

ADVENT

OPENING PRAYER

MARANATHA!
Come, Lord Jesus, come soon!

The glory of God shall be revealed,
and all flesh shall see it together.

Sing aloud, waste places of Jerusalem,
sing to the God who gives courage and strength.
Those who are losing their faith, listen,
and those who are weighed down with failure.
Soon God's salvation will come,
God's deliverance will be revealed.

For a woman shall conceive and bear a son,
and shall call his name Emmanuel, God-with-us.

Hosanna! Blessed is the One
who comes in the name of our God.
Hosanna in the highest!

Maranatha!
Come, Lord Jesus, come soon.

SUNDAY

LET the wilderness and the thirsty land be glad,
let the desert rejoice and burst into flower.
Let the crocus bloom in abundance,
let it rejoice and sing for joy.
The glory, the splendour, of Lebanon, of Carmel,
these too shall see the glory of God.

Strengthen the weary arms, steady the trembling
    knees,
say to the anxious, Be strong, take courage, be not
    afraid.
See, your God comes with true justice:
with dread and doom God comes to save you.

Then the eyes of the blind will be opened,
and the ears of the deaf unstopped;
then shall the lame leap like a deer,
and the tongue of the dumb sing for joy.

For water shall spring up in the desert,
and streams flow in waste land.
The scorched earth will become a lake,
the parched land bubbling springs.

A causeway shall be there, the Holy Way:
nothing unwholesome may travel on it.
It shall be a pilgrim's way: no robber will prowl
    there,
no lion shall devour there, nor any ravenous beast.

But the redeemed shall walk there,
those whom God has rescued will return.
Joy and gladness shall be their escort,
sorrow and sighing shall flee away.
They shall enter the city with shouts of triumph,
crowned with everlasting joy.

THE kingdom of God is at hand:
repent, and believe the Gospel.

> ZION hears the watchmen shouting,
> Her heart leaps up with joy undoubting,
>   She stands and waits with eager eyes;
> See her Friend from heaven descending,
> Adorned with truth and grace unending!
>   Her light burns clear, her star doth rise.
>   Now come, thou precious Crown,
>   Lord Jesus, God's own Son!
>   Hosanna!
>   Let us prepare
>   To follow there,
>   Where in thy supper we may share.

O God, all-powerful in love,
give us grace that we may cast away the works of evil
and put upon us the armour of the good,
now in the time of this earthly life,
in which in Jesus Christ you came to us in great humility,
that on the last day,
when you will reveal yourself to us in greatest glory,
we may rise to the fulness of life eternal,
through the same Jesus Christ,
who lives and reigns with you and the Holy Spirit,
one God, now and for ever.

MONDAY

From the stump of an old gnarled tree,
a new shoot shall yet spring forth.
From roots hidden deep in the ground,
a sapling shall grow again.

The Spirit of God shall rest upon you,
the spirit of wisdom and understanding,
the spirit of counsel and might,
the spirit of knowledge and godly fear.

You will not judge by what your ears hear,
nor decide by what your eyes see.
You will judge the poor with justice,
and defend the humble of the land with equity;
your mouth will be a rod to strike down the ruthless,
and with a word you will devastate the wicked.
Round your waist you will wear the belt of justice,
and good faith will be the girdle round your body.

Then the wolf will dwell with the sheep,
and the leopard lie down with the kid;
the calf and the young lion will grow up together,
and a little child will lead them;
the cow and the bear will feed
and their young will lie down together.

The lion will eat straw like cattle;
the infant will play over the hole of the cobra,
and the young child dance over the viper's nest.

They shall not hurt or destroy in all your holy
    mountain,
for the earth shall be full of the knowledge of God
as the waters cover the sea.

THE night is far spent: the day is at hand.
Let us therefore cast off the works of darkness,
and put on the armour of light.

THOU whose almighty word
Chaos and darkness heard,
    And took their flight;
Hear us, we humbly pray,
And where the gospel day
Sheds not its glorious ray
    Let there be light.

Thou who didst come to bring
On thy redeeming wing
    Healing and sight,
Health to the sick in mind,
Sight to the inly blind,
So now to all our kind
    Let there be light.

Spirit of truth and love,
Life-giving, holy Dove,
    Speed forth thy flight;
Move o'er the water's face,
Bearing the lamp of grace,
And in earth's darkest place
    Let there be light.

Blessed and holy Three,
Glorious Trinity,
   Wisdom, Love, Might,
Boundless as ocean's tide
Rolling in fullest pride,
Through the earth far and wide
   Let there be light.

O GOD, whose love endures beyond the end of the age,
give us grace to bear the nights of darkness,
that we may come at last to see the morning star,
and that you may be born again in us,
so that in the fulfilment of time, on the last great day,
you may come to life in us as the noonday sun,
in the glory of the Christ who lived and loved,
died and rose again for us,
and reigns for ever in your presence.

TUESDAY

COMFORT my people, comfort them, says your God.
Speak tenderly to the city, to Jerusalem,
Your warfare is ended, your iniquity is pardoned,
you have received from God's hand double for all your
   sins.

A voice cries:
In the wilderness prepare the way of Yahweh:
make straight in the desert a highway for our God.
Every valley shall be lifted up,
and every mountain and hill be made low;
the uneven ground shall become level,
and the rough places a plain.
And the glory of the Lord shall be revealed,
for the mouth of the Lord has spoken.

A voice says, Cry!
| And I said, What shall I cry?
All flesh is grass,
and all its beauty is like the flower of the field.
The grass withers, the flower fades,
when the breath of our God blows upon it.
Surely the people is grass.
| The grass withers, the flower fades,
| but the word of our God will stand for ever.

Get you up to a high mountain,
herald of good tidings to Zion;
| lift up your voice with strength,
| herald of good news to Jerusalem:
lift it up, fear not;
say to the cities of Judah,
| Behold your God!

JOHN said, "Behold, the lamb of God, who takes away the sin of the
world. This is he of whom I said, 'After me comes a man who ranks
before me, for he was before me.'"

ON Jordan's bank the Baptist's cry
Announces that the Lord is nigh;
Come then and hearken, for he brings
Glad tidings from the King of kings.

Then cleansed be every human breast,
And furnished for so great a guest!
Yea, let us each our hearts prepare
For Christ to come and enter there.

For thou art our salvation, Lord,
Our refuge and our great reward;
Without thy grace we needs must fade,
And wither like a flower decayed.

Stretch forth thine to heal our sore,
And make us rise, to fall no more;
Once more upon thy people shine,
And fill the world with love divine.

MERCIFUL God,
sending to us your messengers the prophets
to preach repentance and prepare the way for our salvation,
give us grace to heed their warnings,
that we may turn again to you,
and be ready to greet your coming with joy,
in and through Jesus Christ our Saviour.

WEDNESDAY

You are to be praised, O God, in your holy city, .
to you shall vows be honoured, for you answer prayer.
To you shall all flesh come to confess their sins.
When our misdeeds prevail against us,
you will purge them away.

Blessed are those whom you choose
to dwell within your house:
you draw them close to your presence,
and shower upon them rich blessings.

In dread deeds you will deliver us,
O God of our salvation –
you that are the hope of the ends of the earth
and of the distant seas,
who by your strength made fast the mountains –
you that are girded with power,
who stilled the raging of the seas,
the roaring of the waves,
and the tumult of the peoples.

Those who dwell at the ends of the earth
are in awe of your wonders:
the dawn and the evening sing your praise.
You tend the earth and water it,
you make it rich and fertile.
The river of God is full of water:
and you provide grain for the people.
The pastures of the wilderness run over,
and the hills are girded with joy.

The meadows are clothed with sheep,
and the valleys stand so thick with corn
they shout for joy and sing.

Now is the time to wake out of sleep; for now is our salvation
nearer than when we first believed.

COME, thou long-expected Jesus,
    Born to set thy people free,
From our fears and sins release us,
    Let us find our rest in thee.

Israel's strength and consolation,
    Hope of all the earth thou art,
Dear desire of every nation,
    Joy of every longing heart.

Born thy people to deliver,
    Born a child and yet a king,
Born to reign in us for ever,
    Now thy gracious kingdom bring.

By thine own eternal Spirit,
    Rule in all our hearts alone;
By thine all-sufficient merit
    Raise us to thy glorious throne.

O LIVING God, as we wait in these dark days for your coming,
    silent, yearning, expectant,
hope flickering but alight,
place in our hands the lamps of truth and love and courage,
that we may stand firm,
and strive with those powers that rise in the darkness
with their new and strange demands,
that the desires of all our hearts
may be fulfilled in Jesus Christ our Redeemer.

THURSDAY

God, be gracious to us and bless us;
show us the light of your countenance
and be merciful to us,
that your way may be known upon earth,
your saving health among all nations.
  Let the people praise you, O God:
 let all the people praise you.

Let the nations rejoice and be glad,
for you judge the people with justice,
and you guide the nations upon earth.
  Let the people praise you, O God:
 let all the people praise you.

Then shall the earth bring forth her increase,
and God, even our own God,
shall give us great blessing.
  O God, you will bless us indeed,
  and all the ends of the world
 shall praise your holy name.

I saw in my mind's eye a vision:
a new realm, a new order, a new earth;
For the old had decayed and passed away.
Even the sea of chaos had been calmed.
And I saw the holy city, new Jerusalem,
coming out of the clouds of God's presence,
prepared as a bridegroom and bride
adorned as gifts to each other.
I heard the voice of the One who reigns:
Behold, I come to dwell among you, my people,
and you will live in my presence.
I will wipe away every tear from your eyes,
and death shall be no more,
neither shall there be mourning,
nor crying, nor pain, any more.
The former things have passed away:
behold, I make all things new.

THY kingdom come! on bended knee
   The passing ages pray;
And faithful souls have yearned to see
   On earth that kingdom's day.

But the slow watches of the night
   Not less to God belong;
And for the everlasting right
   The silent stars are strong.

And lo, already on the hills
   The flags of dawn appear;
Gird up your loins, ye prophet souls,
   Proclaim the day is near:

The day in whose clear-shining light
   All wrong shall stand revealed,
When justice shall be throned in might,
   And every hurt be healed;

When knowledge, hand in hand with peace,
   Shall walk the earth abroad,
The day of perfect righteousness,
   The promised day of God.

LIVING God,
powerfully in love with us
and with the earth you are creating,
give us such a sense of your presence
that we may turn from our destruction of your world,
and put on the mantle of stewards,
now in the time left to us of this earthly life,
in which, in Jesus Christ, you came to us in great humility,
that on the last and aweful day
when you will reveal yourself to us in terrible and utter beauty,
we shall know the universe transformed to glory;
through the same Jesus,
who dwells for ever in your heart,
vibrant with the Holy Spirit,
one God, now and for ever.

FRIDAY

HEAR, O Shepherd of Israel,
who led Joseph like a flock:
full of radiance in the heavens,
O God, shine out in glory.
Before the least of all your peoples,
stir up your power and come and save us.
| Restore us again, O glorious God,
| show us the light of your countenance
| and we shall be saved.

O God of power and glory,
how long will you be angry with your people?
You have fed us with the bread of tears,
and given us many a bitter drink.
You have made us a victim of our neighbours,
and our enemies laugh us to scorn.
| Restore us again, O glorious God,
| show us the light of your countenance
| and we shall be saved.

Why have you broken down our walls,
so that every passerby can trample us?
The wild beasts of the forest root up the plants,
the very vines that we planted in your name.
Turn to us again, O God of power and glory:
with the eye of your compassion, see.
| Restore us again, O glorious God,
| show us the light of your countenance
| and we shall be saved.

WHEN the Lord comes, he will bring to light things now hidden
in darkness, and will disclose the purposes of the heart.

Lo! God comes with clouds descending,
  Who for sinful folk was slain,
Thousand thousand saints attending,
    Swell the glory of your train:
      Alleluia!
    God is seen on earth to reign.

Every eye shall now behold you,
  Robed in aweful majesty;
We who set at naught and sold you,
    Pierced and nailed you to the Tree,
      Deeply wailing
    Shall our true Messiah see.

Those dear tokens of your passion
  Still your dazzling body bears,
Cause of endless exultation
    To your ransomed worshippers:
      With what rapture
    Gaze we on those glorious scars!

Yea, Amen! Let all adore you,
  Child who once in straw did lie,
Universal praise we give you,
    Reigning now through earth and sky.
      O come quickly!
    Alleluia! Come, Lord, come!

LIVING God, who came among us as a servant,
and refused the panoplies of power,
revealing to us your nature of self-giving love,
so fill us with your Spirit
that we may minister your love in all humility,
sacrificing our selfish desires
for the sake of the well-being of those with whom we have to do,
that through the narrow gate of humdrum service
we may become your tried and trusted friends,
with and in and through Jesus Christ our Saviour.

SATURDAY

O GOD, give wisdom to our rulers,
a sense of justice to those who wield power,
that they may judge your people rightly,
and the poor of the land with equity.
Let the mountains be laden with peace because of their
    wisdom,
and the hills be covered with prosperity for the people.

May they defend the cause of the poor,
save the children of the needy, disarm the oppressor.
May such wisdom endure like the sun and moon,
giving light from age to age.
May justice come down like showers,
watering the new-sown fields.
May wisdom reign from sea to sea,
from the Great River to the ends of the earth.
May folly bow down to truth,
the enemies of justice lick the dust.

For those who are wise deliver the needy when they call,
the poor and those who have no one to speak for them.
They will rescue them from violence and oppression,
and their lives will be precious in their sight.

May prayer be made for them continually,
and blessings invoked on them day by day.
Blessed indeed be the name of our God,
who alone does great wonders.
Blessed be the glorious name of God for ever,
may the whole earth be filled with God's glory.

WHEN I was hungry, you gave me food;
when I was thirsty, you gave me drink;
when I was a stranger, you took me into your home;
when I was naked, you clothed me;
when I was ill, you came to my help;
when I was in prison, you visited me.
As you do these things for the least of your brothers and sisters,
    you do them for me.

For Mary, Mother of the Lord,
  God's holy name be praised,
Who first the Son of God adored,
  As on her child she gazed.

The angel Gabriel brought the word
  She should Christ's mother be,
In simple trust she bore our God,
  And that most willingly.

Herself she offered for God's shrine,
  Her heart to piercing pain,
And knew the cost of love divine
  When Jesus Christ was slain.

Hail, Mary, you are full of grace,
  Above all women blest;
Blest in your Son, whom your embrace
  In birth and death confessed.

Loving God,
calling your friends in new and unexpected ways,
choosing Mary from the powerless and unnoticed in the world,
yet greatly loved and cherished in your sight,
that she should be the mother of our Saviour,
so fill us with your grace
that we too may accept the promptings of your Spirit,
and welcome your angel with glad and open arms,
ready to be pierced with pain and filled with joy,
rejoicing in the cost of your salvation,
in and through the same Jesus our Messiah.

CRIES OF ADVENT

(For each day of December until Christmas Eve)

EACH DAY   Amen! Alleluia! Come, Jesus, Messiah!

You are the Alpha and the Omega,
the first and the last,
the beginning and the end.

Come! say the Spirit and the Bride.
Come! let each hearer reply.
Come forward, all who are thirsty!
Accept the water of life,
a free gift to all who desire it.

You are the descendant of David,
the fulfilment of human hope,
the end of the darkest night,
the bright star of dawn.

The giver of this testimony speaks:
Yes, I am coming soon!

Amen! Alleluia! Come, Jesus, Messiah!

IST   O Living Word,
proceeding from the mouth of God,
penetrating to the ends of the earth,
come and pierce us with the sword of truth.

2ND   O Wisdom,
dwelling in the womb of God,
generating and nurturing the earth through
    nights of darkness,
come and cherish in us the seed of wisdom.

3RD   O Adonai,
ruler of ancient Israel,
appearing to Moses in the flame of the
    burning bush,
carving in him on Sinai the words of living law,
come, etch your holy way even into the lines of
    our faces.

4TH   O Tree of Jesse and Flower of Jesse's Stem,
lifted high as a sign to all the peoples,
before whom even the powerful are struck dumb,
  I come and save us, and delay no more.

5TH   O Key of David and Sceptre of the House of
       Israel
opening where none can shut
and closing what none can open,
  I come and free us, trapped in illusion and the lie.

6TH   O Bright Sun of Justice, Judge of all the world,
seeking to straighten what is crooked
and put right what is wrong,
come with dread power and stark mercy to our
    reluctant hearts.

7TH   O Lion, Regal in Courage,
crushing our blighted bones and hardened hearts,
come with one bound and roar, awaken us, your
    stillborn whelps, to new and vigorous life.

8TH   O Swallow,
capering and darting through the heavens,
ending our winter when you build beneath our
    eaves,
come, bird from paradise, small and powerless,
    invincible as the phoenix.

9TH   O Cornerstone, O Keystone of the Arch,
holding in your being the opposites of your creation,
come and give us courage in our bearing and our
    striving.

10TH   O Sovereign Stag, of Hind Embracing,
fresh and whole and eager,
carrying love's immortal wound,
come to us who are banished, barren, snared;
climb down to free us;
lead us home to headwaters, crags, and
    columbines.

IITH   O Salmon,
        leaping like lightning from the womb,
        bursting above cascades of chaos,
        climbing love's deadly ladder,
        come and sow your blood and burning water at
            the ancient source of all our sorrow:
        drowning, you destroy our death;
        leaping, you lead us to life:
        O Ichthus, come in glory.

12TH   O Sovereign of all the Peoples,
        uniting Jew and Gentile, white and black,
        come and reconcile us whom you are shaping out
            of common clay.

13TH   O Divine Eagle,
        soaring in the skies,
        shadow gliding across the valley floor,
        come and hover over us, your brood,
        who pierced the only pinions
            that can bear us up from death and sin
            to sun and moon and eternal life.

14TH   O Voice of the Voiceless,
        enabling to find words those whom others have
            made speechless,
        come and lift the outcast from the dungeons of
            their silence.

15TH   O Wounded Healer,
        enduring in the heart of God,
        enfolding the universe in strong and gentle hands,
        come and soothe our flesh with astringent balm.

16TH   O Morning Star, Splendour of Light Eternal,
        O Radiant Dawn, O Dayspring from on high,
        shining with the glory of the rainbow,
        come and waken us from the greyness of our
            apathy,
        and renew in us your gift of hope.

17TH O Passionate Lover,
    stirring in the loins of God,
    yearning to create what is ever new,
  | come and open our flesh to love's fierce touch.

18TH O Anointed One, Long-awaited Messiah,
    blessing, healing, and commissioning your people,
  | come and empower us to serve your purpose of
      liberating love.

19TH O Emmanuel, God-with-us,
    at one with our humanity,
    whose glory is our abundant life,
  | come and transform us who find our destiny in
      you.

20TH O Music of the Spheres, O Song of Silence,
    echoing through ears that listen,
  | come with still small voice and heal.

21ST O Midnight Star,
    leading the way through the desert to the
      promised land,
  | come and carry the covenant in your flesh
  | and lead us through the thorns of love.

22ND O Girl-Child, O Boy-Child,
    free and unreserved,
    laughing in play through the cosmos,
  | come and leap into our hearts in joy.

23RD O Child of God,
    calling together the creatures of the earth,
    the vulnerable with the powerful,
  | come, gentle our strength,
  | coax our trembling into song.

24TH O Unicorn,
    creature of our dreams,
    quivering, fierce, and tender,
  | come in the dead of night with new-born cry.

EACH DAY   Maranatha!
Come, Lord Jesus, come soon!
Christ has come!
Christ comes now!
Christ will come!
Alleluia!

CHRISTMAS

OPENING PRAYER

BLESSED be God who alone works wonders!
Blessed for ever be God's glorious name!

Through the tender mercy of our God
the day has dawned upon us from on high
to give light to those who sit in darkness
    and in the shadow of death,
and to guide our feet in ways of peace.

Living Word of Light and Love,
you became a human being,
you pitched your tent among us,
and lived the fulness of our humanity,
full of grace and truth.

A Child is born to us, alleluia!
A Son is given to us, alleluia!
All the ends of the earth
have seen the salvation of our God.
Alleluia! Alleluia!

ODD-NUMBERED DAYS

We praise you, O God, holy and beloved!
I We praise you for your glory and wisdom!
We praise you for your marvellous deeds!
I We praise you in the sound of the trumpet!
We praise you upon the flute and harp!
I We praise you in the cymbals and dances!
We praise you on the strings and pipe!
I We praise you on the deep resounding drums!
We praise you in the Infant Jesus!
We praise you, Emmanuel, God-with-us!
Let everything that breathes under the sun
on this glad day give you praise!
Alleluia! Alleluia!

ETERNAL Word, with God from the beginning,
in whom and through whom everything has come to be,
in you is life, the life that is our light,
the light that shines on in the darkness,
which the darkness has never overcome,
the true light, enlightening us all, shining in the world.
Yet we did not recognize you.
You came to your own people – and we knew you not.
You came to your own home – and we received you not.
But to those who did, who believed in your name,
you gave power to become your children,
to be known as your servants and your friends,
born not of the will of flesh and blood,
but of the desire of your love.
Living Word of Light and Love, you were made flesh;
you came to dwell among us, full of grace and truth.
We saw your glory,
divine glory shining through a human face,
as a mother's eyes live through her daughter's,
as a son reflects his father's image,
your glory in a human being fully alive.

O GOD our Redeemer,
you have delivered us from the dominion of evil and pain,
and brought us in your beloved Christ
into the realm of goodness and healing.
You have rescued us from the bands of slavery,
you have forgiven all our failure to love.

For Christ is the image of your invisible being,
the first-born of all creation,
in whom the universe is being made,
the earth and the sun and the other stars,
things visible and things invisible,
through whom and for whom all things were formed,
who is before all things,
and in whom all things hold together.

Christ is the head of the body, the Church,
the beginning, the first-born from the dead.

For it pleased you, O God,
that in Christ all fulness should dwell,
and through Christ all things be reconciled to yourself.

CHRISTIANS awake! Salute the happy morn
Whereon the Saviour of the world was born:
Rise to adore the mystery of love
Which hosts of angels chanted from above;
With them the joyful tidings first begun
Of God incarnate and the Virgin's Son.

Like Mary let us ponder in our mind
God's wondrous love in saving humankind;
Trace we the Babe, who has retrieved our loss,
From the poor manger to the bitter cross;
Tread in his steps, assisted by his grace,
Till our true heavenly state indeed takes place.

EVEN-NUMBERED DAYS

WE praise you, O God,
with heart and soul we praise you.
While we live we will praise you, O God,
while we have any being
we will sing praises to our God.

Put not your trust in rulers,
nor in the children of earth, who cannot save.
For when their breath goes from them
they return again to the earth,
and on that day all their thoughts perish.

Blessed are those whose help is the God of Jacob,
whose hope is in Yahweh their God,
the God who is making the heavens and the earth,
the seas and all that is in them,
who keeps faith for ever,
who deals justice to those who are oppressed.

For you give food to the hungry, O God,
and you set the captives free.
You give sight to the blind,
you lift up those who are bowed down.
You love the humble poor,
you care for the stranger in the land.
You uphold the widow and the orphan,
and as for way of the wicked you turn it upside down.

You have fulfilled your covenant with the earth,
being born as one of us, flesh of our flesh,
that we may become as you are, made whole in your love,
that the universe itself be transfigured to glory.

MARY kept all these things, pondering them in her heart. And the
shepherds returned, glorifying and praising God for all that they
had heard and seen, as it had been told them.

THE people who walked in darkness
have seen a great light;
those who dwelt in a land of deep darkness,
upon them has the light dawned.

As a child you have been born to us,
as a son you have been given to us:
Wonderful Counsellor, Creator God,
Beloved Abba, Harbinger of Peace.
From the days of our ancestors of faith,
in fulfilment of the covenants of promise,
your Word of Love has struggled to be born,
and at last is made clear in the Word made flesh.

WHERE is this stupendous stranger?
Prophets, shepherds, kings, advise:
Lead me to my Master's manger,
Show me where my Saviour lies.

O most mighty, O most holy,
 Far beyond the seraph's thought!
Art thou then so mean and lowly
 As unheeded prophets taught?

O the magnitude of meekness,
 Worth from worth immortal sprung!
O the strength of infant weakness,
 If eternal is so young!

God all-bounteous, all creative,
 Whom no ills from good dissuade,
Is incarnate – and a native
 Of the very world he made.

PRAYER ON EACH DAY

LET us rejoice in the Mystery of the Incarnation, in the Humanity of God, in the Wonder of the Word made Flesh.

Let us rejoice that God is with us, a hidden silent presence transforming to gold the leaden rock of earth.

Let us rejoice that the best name of God is Love, a Love that draws us like a magnet, that nothing can defeat, neither evil nor pain nor death.

Let us rejoice in God revealed to us as a baby, whose weakness is stronger than our brittle pride, whose light shines clearer than our wilful blindness.

Let us rejoice that God has given us one another, that we might learn to bear the beams of love.

Let us pray that we may not betray God's trust in us, nor our own in one another.

Let us pray that we may have courage to change our lives, as nations and as individuals, that the hungry may be fed, the poor achieve dignity, the oppressed go free, and the stranger be welcomed.

Let us pray for those in authority among us, that they may respect
the law and seek to reform it, and work for justice and the
common good.

Let us pray for the peacemakers of the world and all who through
their vision and struggle seek to make us citizens of one earth.

Let us remember the lonely and anxious among us, the old, the
homeless and the hungry, the foolish and the despairing, the sick
at heart and those in pain, the dying and those who mourn, and
those whose hearts are hardened against the love of God.

Let us remember those who rejoice with us, but upon another
shore and in a greater light, that multitude that no one can
number, whose hope was in the Word made flesh, and with
whom, in this, we for evermore are one.

ETERNAL and loving God,
wonderfully creating us in your own image,
striving with our reluctant wills,
renewing us in Jesus when we fail to love,
so fill us with your Spirit
that as he came to share in our humanity,
we may come to share in his divinity;
who is alive and reigns with you and the Holy Spirit,
one God, now and for ever. Amen.

Christ, who by your incarnation
gathered into one things earthly and heavenly,
fill us with your joy and peace,
now and for ever. Amen.

EPIPHANY

OPENING PRAYER

THE grace of God has appeared
for the salvation of all people.

Lift up your eyes, O City of God, and see:
people coming together,
gathering before your gates.
So you shall know and be glad,
your heart shall thrill and rejoice.

Arise, shine, Jerusalem, for your light has come,
and the glory of God has risen upon you.

Glory to God in the highest, alleluia!
On earth peace to folk of goodwill, alleluia!
All the ends of the earth have seen
the salvation of our God, alleluia!

ODD-NUMBERED DAYS

MY heart is aflame with fine phrases,
I make my song for the great king:
my tongue is the pen of a ready writer.

You are the fairest of the children of earth:
grace flows from your lips:
therefore God has blessed you for ever and ever.

We praise you, O God,
for the gift of yourself in the Infant King:
Jesus, Sovereign Ruler of all,
in whom is our royal destiny too:
celebrants at the banquet of heaven,
guests at the great marriage feast,
gloriously singing in triumphal procession,
our ancestors and descendants with us,
joyful in the communion of your saints.

Dear God, we bring the offering of ourselves this day,
the gift of love in our hearts and our loins,
the incense of prayer, the myrrh of our suffering,
the gold of all that we hold most dear,
that you may create through our loyal obedience
such wonders as pass our imagining.
Alleluia, alleluia, alleluia!

WHEN the wise men had heard the king, they went their way; and
lo, the star which they had seen in the East went before them, till
it came and stood over where the child was. When they saw the star
they rejoiced exceedingly with great joy; and going into the house
they saw the child with Mary his mother, and they fell down and
worshipped him. Then, opening their treasures, they offered him
gifts, gold, and frankincense, and myrrh. And being warned in a
dream not to return to Herod, they departed to their own country
another way.

EVEN-NUMBERED DAYS

O CLAP your hands, all you peoples:
cry aloud to God with shouts of joy.
Approach the presence of God with awe,
the great Sovereign over all the earth.

O God, you have called us to serve the peoples,
that they may come to acknowledge your glory.
You have made us stewards of your gifts,
that we may not boast and be proud.
You have loved us and blessed us with a goodly
    heritage,
overflowing with all that we need.

Let us join the procession in praise of your name,
with trumpets and horns and the sound of rejoicing.
We sing praises, sing praises to you, O God,
we sing praises, sing praises to your name.

For you are the Sovereign over all the earth.
Let us praise you with well-wrought psalm.
You are the Ruler of all the peoples,
wise and just in your dealings.

Those who give counsel gather together
as the people of the God of Abraham.
For even the mighty ones of the earth
are become the servants of God,
the God who is greatly to be praised.

JESUS rejoiced in the Holy Spirit and said, "I thank thee, Father, Lord of heaven and earth, that thou hast hidden these things from the wise and understanding, and revealed them to babes; yes, Father, for such was thy gracious will. All things have been delivered to me by my Father; and no one knows who is the Son except the Father, or who the Father is except the Son and any one to whom the Son chooses to reveal him."

CANTICLE, HYMN, AND PRAYER FOR EACH DAY

Refrain The city has no need of sun or moon
　　　　to shine upon it,
　　for the glory of God is its light,
　　and its lamp is the Lamb.

ARISE, shine, for your light has come,
and the glory of God is shining upon you,
even though darkest night still covers the earth,
and thick darkness the peoples . . .

God will arise upon you,
and God's glory will be seen among you,
and nations shall come to your light,
rulers to the brightness of your rising . . .

The sun shall no more be your light by day,
nor shall the moon give light to you by night,
for God will be your everlasting light,
and your God will be your glory . . .

O WORSHIP the Lord in the beauty of holiness,
　Bow down before him, his glory proclaim;
With gold of obedience and incense of lowliness,
　Kneel and adore him: the Lord is his name.

Low at his feet lay thy burden of carefulness,
　High on his heart he will bear it for thee,
Comfort thy sorrows, and answer thy prayerfulness,
　Guiding thy steps as may best for thee be.

Fear not to enter his courts in the slenderness
　Of the poor wealth thou wouldst reckon as thine;
Truth in its beauty, and love in its tenderness,
　These are the offerings to lay on his shrine.

These, though we bring them in trembling and fearfulness,
　He will accept for the name that is dear;
Mornings of joy give for evenings of tearfulness,
　Trust for our trembling, and hope for our fear.

Refrain   . . . let the Light of Christ shine.

In the dark cells of our hearts. . .
In the dark alleys of our cities. . .
In the rejected places within us. . .
In the dank cold of our estrangements. . .
In the dark space between the stars. . .
On the blindness of our foolishness. . .
In the darkness where murder is plotted. . .
In the dark caves where missiles lurk. . .

Eternal God, Light of the Universe,
revealed as utter and unfailing Love
in Jesus of Nazareth, a man and a Jew,
still draw us to yourself as you have drawn so many,
men and women, Jews and Gentiles,
shepherds and wise men, nomads and settlers,
that human beings everywhere may embrace one another,
and the whole world at last reflect your glory.

LENT

OPENING PRAYER

FOOLS to the world, we know the wisdom of God.
Unknown, we cannot be ignored.
Dying, we still live on.
Disciplined by suffering, we are not beaten down.
Knowing sorrow, we have always cause for joy.
Poor ourselves, we make many rich.
Penniless, we own the world.

Steadfastly we turn our wills towards God,
to meet hardships and afflictions,
hunger and weariness, illness and failure,
with sincerity, insight, patience, kindness,
speaking the truth in love,
resilient in the power of the Spirit.

SUNDAY

AT the turning of the day I make ready for my prayer,
emptying my mind, opening my heart,
my whole self watching and waiting.
Out of the silence comes my cry,
the groaning of my spirit, profound, beyond words.

O God my Deliverer, listen, and answer.
You take no delight in wickedness,
evil may not sojourn with you.
The boastful may not stand before your eyes,
the proud wither at your glance.
Your silence those who speak lies,
you withstand the thrust of the vengeful.

Only through the gift of your steadfast love
do I dare to enter your presence.
I will worship in your holy house
in trembling and awe.

So easy it is to fall in false ways –
lead me, O God, in your justice,
make my path straight before me.
For there is no truth in our mouths,
our hearts are set on destruction,
our throats are an open sepulchre,
we flatter with our tongue.

Our speeches are honeyed with peace,
smooth words slide from our lips.
the wavelengths dance with lies,
siren songs deceive in the dark.

Make us together feel the burden of our sin,
let us fall by the weight of our deceits,
crumbling by reason of our trespass,
lost because of our rebellion.

Pluck us from the despair that follows the lie,
no longer weighed down with the burden of falsehood.
Strengthen our steps in obedience to truth,
turn our lamentation to dancing and joy.
Set us on fire with unquenchable love:
we shall honour your name, exulting with praise.

BLESSED be God,
who showers blessings on the just and the unjust.
Blessed be God,
enduring with us the showers of black rain.
Blessed be God,
shuddering with pain when sirens wail.
Blessed be God,
our blasts but a feather in the wind of the Spirit.
Blessed be God,
our evil but a drop in the ocean of Love.
Blessed be God,
redeeming our wastes and our sorrows.
Blessed be God.

JESUS said, "Truly I say to you, unless a grain of wheat falls into the earth and dies, it remains alone; but if it dies, it bears much fruit. If you love your life you will lose it, and if you hate your life in this world, you will keep it for eternal life. If you would serve me, you must follow me; and where I am, there shall my servant be also; if you serve me, the Father will honour you."

WE turn our faces towards you, O God,
for you have torn us and you will heal us,
you have stricken us and you will bind up our wounds.
After two days you will revive us,
on the third day you will raise us up,
that we may live in your presence and praise you.
Let us humble ourselves, let us strive to know you, O God,
for your justice dawns like the morning light,
its dawning sure as the sunrise.
You will come to us like the spring rains,
like the gentle showers that water the earth.

OUR desires are corrupted and warped.
In the depth of our being we long for our idols:
they are but a reflection of our self-concern.
Loving God, turn around our hearts and our faces:
let us worship you, the Living Truth.
We exploit others for what we want from them.
Loving God, straighten what is twisted within us:
let us serve the needs of our neighbours.
We acquire possessions to hide our insecurity.
Loving God, hold back our greedy hands:
let us delight in the gifts you have given to all.

MONDAY

WHY do the nations rage at one another?
Why do we plot and conspire?
The powerful of the earth set themselves high,
and the people collude with their pride.
They whisper against God's Anointed,
chosen to embody God's will.

Be not mocked or derided, O God:
speak to us in your wrath,
terrify us in your fury,
break us with your rod of iron,
dash us in pieces like a potter's vessel,
bring us in fear and trembling
to fall down before you and kiss your feet.

But who *is* this, God's Chosen One, God's *Son*?
Inheritor of the earth and all its people?
You take the rage of all our hearts upon yourself,
mocked and crucified, yet meeting all with love.

Ah, Fire that shrivels up our hates,
and brings us to our knees in awe!
Ah, Love that pierces all our fury,
laying bare our greed and pride!
Forgive us, for we know not what we do.

JESUS said, "The light is with you for a little longer. Walk while you
have the light, lest the darkness overtake you; if you walk in the
darkness you do not know where you go. While you have the light,
believe in the light, that you may become children of light."

O MY people, what shall I do with you?
Your love for me is like the morning mist,
like the dew that vanishes early.

So I have hewn you by my prophets,
and my judgment goes forth like a laser.
For I desire loyalty and not mere ritual,
the knowledge of myself, not dumb mouthings.

When you were a child, I loved you:
out of your enslavement I called you.
I taught you to walk, I took you in my arms,
even when you did not know that it was I who healed you.
I led you with cords of compassion, with the bands of love.
I became to you as one who eases the yoke on your shoulders,
and I bent down to you and fed you.

Yet still you rebel against me, and refuse to return to me.
You turn away in stubbornness and pride,
and bring the wrath of my Love upon yourselves.

But I cannot give you up to destruction,
I cannot hand you over to the power of death.
My heart recoils within me,
my compassion grows warm and tender,
and I will not execute my fierce anger,
I will not destroy you.
For I am God and not as the peoples.
I am the Holy One in your midst,
and I will not come to destroy.

> PUNCTURE my bloated pride:
> I sow the hidden seed of humility.
>   Root out my cruel and bitter anger:
> I sow the hidden seed of courtesy.
>   Disentangle me from the web of envy:
> I sow the hidden seed of justice.
>   Make clear the hypocrisies of my lust:
> I sow the hidden seed of truth.
>   Take from my heart my grasping after money:
> I sow the hidden seed of generosity.
>   Still my gluttonous pursuit of pleasure:
> I sow the hidden seed of charity.
>   Penetrate the fog of my sloth:
> I sow the hidden seed of laughter.

TUESDAY

Do you decree what is just, O rulers of the nations?
Do you with justice judge the peoples?
No, you work in the land with evil heart,
you look on the violence your hands have wrought.

The wicked are estranged even from the womb,
they are liars that go astray from their birth.
They are venomous with the venom of serpents,
like the deaf asp that stops its ears
and will not heed the voice of the charmer,
though the binder of spells be skilful.

Break their teeth, O God, in their mouths,
shatter the jaws of the young lions, O God.
Let them vanish like water that drains away,
let them be trodden down and wither like grass,
like an abortive birth that sees not the sun.
Let them be cut down like thorns before they know it,
like brambles which are swept angrily aside.

The just shall rejoice when they see your vengeance,
they will wash their feet in the blood of the wicked.
People will say, There is a reward for the virtuous,
there is indeed a God who judges the earth . . .

Purge me, O God, of malice and hatred,
cleanse my soul from bitterness of memory,
stop my rejoicing at the pain of their doom,
even those who have persecuted me most.

Only so can I hope to stand in your presence,
for you read all my ways and my heart,
all its murky unease and its fickleness.
We are all unjust, disordered, and lawless,
hardly sensing the lure of your love.
We can but sense it as wrath.

Withhold your light – it will blind us,
yet let us not perish in the dark and the cold.
Warm by degrees the hearts that are frozen,
till the depths of the darkness dazzle.

Have mercy upon us, have mercy,
criminals and judges knowing the roughest of justice.
No plea can we enter before you.
It is the deprived and homeless, the ragged and
    shivering,
who stand in the court to accuse us.
Those on the edge, the unkempt, unacceptable,
they are the ones who show us your face.
And, deep within, is a child who is shunned,
whom we treat as our enemy, battered and bruised.

O when will we learn to stretch our our arms,
to receive from the outcasts and scapegoats
the redeeming embrace and the melting of tears:
⎮ in these and these only is our last dying hope.

JESUS said, "I am the true vine, and my Father is the vinedresser.
Every branch of mine that bears no fruit, he takes away, and every
branch that does bear fruit he prunes, that it may bear more fruit."

O GOD of our ancestors, blessed be your name for ever!
Yours is the greatness, the power, and the glory,
the majestic and marvellous splendour.
For everything in the heavens and on the earth is yours.
From your hand come all the blessings of life,
open gifts of goods and honour,
secret gifts in pain and dying.
Even in the midst of change and decay,
O God, you reign for ever and ever.
You pour out your life in love for us,
even to weakness, emptiness, and dread,
yearning for us to respond,
drawing us closer to your presence.
And so we give you thanks, O God,
and praise your glorious name,
for all things come from you
and of your own do we give you.

ABBA, strengthen us in your service,
alert us to your will,
consecrate us in the truth,
enlighten our minds,
warm our hearts,
channel our emotions,
give grace to our flesh,
fill us with courage,
expose us to the truth of our hidden selves,
keep us obedient to the Spirit within,
loyal to our greatest awareness of truth.

WEDNESDAY

O God, the foundation of my hope,
you are the ground of my trust.
May I not be disappointed in my days,
may the powers of oppression fade away.

Show me your ways, O God,
and teach me your paths.
Lead me in your truth and guide me,
for you are the God of my salvation.

I have hoped in you all the day long,
because of your goodness and faithfulness,
your steadfast love to your people,
streaming towards us from days of old.

Remember not the sins of my youth,
nor my trespass and trampling on others.
According to your mercy think on me,
call to mind your agelong compassion.

You are full of justice and grace:
you guide sinners in the Way.
You lead the humble to do what is right,
filled with the gentle strength of the meek.
All your paths are faithful and true,
for those who are loyal to your covenant.

For your name's sake, O God,
be merciful to me, for my sin is great.
I come to you in trembling and awe:
guide me in the way I should choose.

My eyes look towards you, O God,
and you free me from the snares of the net.
Turn your face to me –
it is full of your grace and your love.

For I am lonely and in misery,
my heart is in pain and constricted:
the arteries of affection are hardened.
Open me wide and lift my heart high,
the breath of your Spirit filling my lungs.

Take to yourself my wretched affliction,
bring me out of my distress,
and forgive all my sins.
See how strong are the powers of oppression,
eyes full of hatred and violence.

Guard my life and deliver me,
clothe me with integrity and love.
Bring me to the innocence that no longer harms,
for you are my strength and salvation.
I wait for you: you are my hope.
May I never shrink away in shame.

JESUS said, "As the Father has loved me, so I have loved you; abide in my love. If you keep my commandments, you will abide in my love, just as I have kept my Father's commandments and abide in his love. These things I have spoken to you, that my joy may be in you, and that your joy may be full."

O GOD, I seek you while you may be found,
I call upon you while you are near.
May I forsake all wicked ways,
and refuse all thoughts of injustice.
I turn again to you, O God,
that you may have mercy upon me.
O God, you are my Redeemer,
abundant in forgiveness and love.

Your thoughts are not our thoughts,
neither are your ways our ways.
As the rain and snow come down from the skies,
and return not again but water the earth,
bringing forth life and giving growth,
seed for the sowing and bread for the eating,

so the Word that goes forth from your mouth
will not return to you empty.
But it will accomplish that which your purpose,
and succeed in the task that you give it.

LET us embrace the Way of the Crucified Jesus:
fountain of life,
source of hope,
deliverer from slavery,
maker of peace,
obedient to death,
pioneer of the narrow way,
burning flame of love,
source of all faithfulness,
santuary of justice,
elder brother,
Lamb slain from before the foundation of the world,
bodily presence of the fulness of God,
our life, our death, our resurrection.

THURSDAY

"GIVE judgment for me, O God:
for I have walked in my integrity,
I have trusted you without wavering.
Put me to the test and try me:
examine my mind and my heart.
For your steadfast love is before my eyes,
and I have walked in your truth.

I have not sat with deceivers,
nor consorted with hypocrites;
I hate the company of evildoers,
and I will not sit with the wicked.

I wash my hands in innocence, O God,
that I may approach your altar,
lifting up the voice of thanksgiving,
and telling of all your marvellous deeds.
Dear God, I love the house of your dwelling,
the place where your glory shines.

Do not sweep me away with sinners,
nor my life with people of blood,
who murder with their evil weapons,
and whose hands are full of bribes.
As for me I walk in my integrity:
redeem me and be gracious to me.
My foot stands on firm ground:
I will bless you in the great congregation."

Who in this world of ours now
can dare take that prayer as their own?
Perhaps the ones imprisoned for conscience,
persecuted and tortured for faith,
tempted to renounce their beliefs,
holding firm to the most sacred of vows.
Yet even the greatest of saints
knows no boast in the presence of God.
Kyrie eleison, Christe eleison, Kyrie eleison.

Forgive the boast of your people, O God,
self-righteous and blind in our mouthings.
We have not done a tenth of these things,
nor dare we plead any innocence.
We project the evil of our hearts on to others,
and destroy our enemies in your cause.
The drumbeat of the psalmist has sounded
through the years of inquisitions and war.
Kyrie eleison, Christe eleison, Kyrie eleison.

JESUS said, "This is my commandment, that you love one another
as I have loved you. Greater love has no one than this, than to lay
down one's life for one's friends. You are my friends if you do what
I command you. No longer do I call you servants, for the servant
does not know what his master is doing; but I have called you
friends, for all that I have heard from my Father I have made
known to you."

How blest the meek! How blest the poor in spirit!
God's Commonwealth is their heritage,
and their inheritance the earth.

How blest the mourners! How blest are they that weep!
| For they shall laugh and shall be comforted.

How blest are they that thirst for righteousness,
and they that hunger after holiness!
| They shall be satisfied.

How blest the merciful!
| They shall themselves be judged with mercy and
    compassion.

How blest the pure in heart!
| They shall see the face of God.

How blest the peacemakers!
| They are the daughters and the sons of God.

And blest are they
who for the sake of righteousness are persecuted!
| The Freedom of the City of God is theirs.

SPIRIT of Wisdom,
take from us all fuss,
the clattering of noise,
the temptation to dominate by the power of words,
the craving for certainty.
| Lead us through the narrow gate of not knowing,
| that we may listen and obey,
| and come to a place of stillness,
| of true conversation and wisdom.

Spirit of Love,
take from us all lust,
the battering of force,
the temptation to dominate by physical power,
the craving for control.
| Lead us through the narrow gate of loneliness,
| that we may be chaste and let others be,
| and come to a place of intimacy,
| of deep communion and love.

Spirit of Freedom,
take from us all rust,
the cluttering of things,
the temptation to dominate by the power of money,
the craving for comfort.
Lead us through the narrow gate of constriction,
that we may let go of possessions,
and come to a place of simplicity,
of glad conviviality and freedom.

FRIDAY

BLESSED are those whose sin is forgiven,
the trace of whose trespass is erased.
Blessed are those whom God does not blame,
in whose heart is no guile.

I kept my secret sins to myself,
I refused to bring them to light.
My energy wasted away,
my days were full of complaint,
a grumble murmuring in my ears.
Day and night your hand was heavy upon me:
the flow of my being became sluggish and dry,
like parched land in the drought of summer.

Then I acknowledged my sin in your presence:
I hid no longer from myself or from you.
I said, "I will confess my evil to God."
So you released me from the guilt of my sin.
For this cause all those who are faithful
pray in their hearts in the day of their troubles.
Even in times of overwhelming distress,
with the thunder and force of waters in flood,
your grace is for me like a temple of rock,
standing firm in the face of the powers,
ordering the discord and chaos within,
preserving my life from utter destruction.
In the eye of the storm I hear the whisper of mercy,
the peace of those who are completely forgiven.

"I will instruct you and guide you,
I will teach you the way you should go.
I will counsel you with my ear to the truth,
a keen and kindly eye fixed upon you.
Do not be like horse or mule with no understanding,
whose course must be curbed with bridle and bit."

Many are the pangs of the wicked:
steadfast love surounds those who trust God.
People of integrity, rejoice in God and be glad:
shout for joy all you that are true of heart.

In Christ we pray:
Bapu, I give you praise,
Lover of the world,
the learned and the wise
have missed the secrets of your heart.
It is the way of simplicity itself,
and it is the simple who find it.
Yes, Bapu, I give you the glory.

Come to me,
all whose work is hard,
whose load is heavy.
I will refresh you
and give you relief.
Bend your necks to my yoke,
and I will show you how to live.
I will go your pace
and see you through,
and give you the secret
of a quiet mind.
For I am gentle
and humble of heart.
Pulling the yoke with me is easy,
the load with my help is light.

LET us be fools for Christ's sake:
in facing the truth, may we be set free from illusion;
in accepting our wounds, may we be healed and made whole;
in embracing the outcast, may be know ourselves redeemed;
in discovering our child, may we grow to full stature;
in seeking true innocence, may we no longer harm;
in yielding to dying, may abundant life flow into us;
in vulnerable risk, may we know love's pain and joy;
in the folly of the Cross, may we see the Wisdom of God.

SATURDAY

THE web of the world trembles,
the whisper of a great wind passing.
The caressing of strings makes music,
its sighs reach the ends of the world.
The stars in the heaven chant the glory of God,
pulsing their praise across aeons of space.

From the soft radiance of a summer dawn
to the stormy sunset of a winter's evening,
from the darkest and wildest of mountain nights
to the stillness of moonlit seas,
the voice of praise is never silent,
yet all without speech or language
or sound of any voice.

So too with the mighty sun,
come forth as a bridegroom from his tent,
rejoicing at his wedding day,
exulting in youthful splendour and beauty.
He climbs the sky from the eastern horizon,
he declines to the west at the end of the day,
and nothing can escape the fire of his presence.

Galaxies beyond take up the cry,
suns ever more brilliant and huge:
Arcturus twenty times the size of Earth's sun,
Sigma in Dorado hundreds of thousands,
Aldebaran millions of miles in diameter:
all, all proclaim the glory of God.

The law of God is perfect,
I refreshing the soul.
  The words of God are sure,
I and give wisdom to the simple.
  The justice of God is righteous,
I and rejoices the heart.
  The commandment of God is pure,
I and gives light to the eyes.
  The fear of God is clean,
I and endures for ever.
  The judgments of God are true,
I and just in every way.

So they dance as the stars of the universe,
perfect as the parabolas of comets,
like satellites and planets in their orbits,
reliable and constant in their courses.

The Wisdom of God – more to be desired than gold,
sweeter than syrup and honey from the comb.
And by her is your servant taught,
in the very keeping of the Law there is great reward.

Who can tell how often I offend?
Cleanse me from my secret faults.
Keep your servant from pride and conceit,
lest they get the dominion over me.
So may I stand in your presence,
innocent of great offence.
Let the words of my mouth
and the meditations of my heart
be always acceptable in your sight,
O God, my strength and my redeemer.

JESUS said: "I pray for those whom thou hast given me, not that thou shouldst take them out of the world, but that thou shouldst keep them from the evil one. They are not of the world, even as I am not of the world. Sanctify them in the truth; thy word is truth. As thou didst send me into the world, so I have sent them into the world. And for their sake I consecrate myself, that they also may be consecrated in truth."

You are the Bread of Life:
  those who come to you shall not hunger,
  those who trust you shall never thirst.

You are the Living Bread:
  those who eat of you shall live for ever,
  knowing the secret of a life that nothing can destroy.

The Bread that you give is your life,
  given for the life of the world.

  Unless we feed on you we have no life in us.
  Let us eat your flesh and drink your blood,
  and so abide in you and you in us,
  and know the secret of eternal life.

LET us reflect on the vows of Baptism:

Are we willing to turn again to Christ,
to turn to the deep things of God,
to the Spirit of God moving within us and among us,
to God the Source and Goal of all that is,
to the Mysterious Companion who is the Other within us,
to Christ, truly divine and truly human,
living the way of unconditional love?

Are we willing day by day to turn our hearts and minds
in repentance towards the God of Love,
confessing our failures to love,
forgiving ourselves and others
and allowing ourselves to be forgiven,
absorbing hurts
and not passing them on in a spirit of retaliation?

Are we willing to refuse the way of evil,
of self-hatred and the hatred of others,
to keep steadfastly to the true path,
the Way, the Truth, and the Life of Jesus,
to refuse the easy and comfortable way of unawareness of all
    that is pressing upon us,
rather embracing and participating in the way of compassion?

PASSIONTIDE

FIRST DAY

JESUS became obedient to death, even death on a cross.

> YOU grew up before us like a young plant,
> with roots in arid ground.
> You had no grace or beauty
> that would delight our eyes.
> You were disfigured and rejected,
> sorrowful, acquainted with grief.
>
> We turned our faces from you,
> you became as refuse in our sight.
>
> Yet you bore our sickness and grief,
> you endured our sorrow and pain.
>
> and we thought you were punished by God,
> struck down by disease and misery.
>
> But you were scourged for our faults,
> you were bruised for our sins.
>
> On you lies the chastisement that makes us whole,
> and with your wounds we are healed.

GOD has shown his love for us in that while we were yet sinners,
Christ died for us.

> HAVE mercy upon me, O God,
> for I am distressed and in pain:
> no one hears the cry of my loneliness.
> My eyes have become dimmed with grief,
> the whole of me body and soul.
> My life is worn away with sorrow,
> and my years with mourning.
> My strength fails me because of my affliction,
> and my bones are wasting away.

I am the scorn of all my enemies,
and a burden to my neighbours.
My acquaintances, they are afraid of me;
when they see me in the street they shrink away.
I am clean forgotten, like a dead man out of mind;
I have become like a broken vessel.
For I hear the conspiring of many,
the whispering of threats on every side,
as they plot to take away my life.

The hope of my days is in your hands:
I trust you, my God, "Thou that art Thou."
Deliver me from the power of my enemies,
from the grip of those who persecute me.
Show your servant the light of your countenance
and save me in your steadfast love.

Let me not be confounded, O God,
for I have called upon you.
Let ungodliness be put to confusion,
and brought to silence in the grave.
Let lying lips be made dumb,
the voices of cruelty and pride
that speak with spite against the just.

How great is your goodness towards us, O God,
poured out on the just and the unjust,
yet received and known
in the depths of a trusting heart.
Rescue us from all that conspires against us,
even the betrayals of hearts and lips:
shelter us in your refuge from the strife of tongues.

O God, I give you thanks
for you have shown me marvellous great kindness.
When I was alarmed, like a city besieged,
I felt cut off from your sight.
Nevertheless, you heard the voice of my prayer
when I cried to you for help.

All your servants love you, O God,
for you enfold us in your faithfulness,
and retrieve us sternly when we are proud.
With firmness of will and courage of heart,
we will follow your way,
trusting that you are our God,
our faithful Creator and Friend.

SINCE, in the wisdom of God, the world did not know God through wisdom, it pleased God through the folly of what we preach to save those who believe. For Jews demand signs and Greeks seek wisdom, but we preach Christ crucified, a stumbling block to Jews and folly to Gentiles, but to those who are called, both Jews and Greeks, Christ the power of God and the wisdom of God. For the foolishness of God is wiser than human wisdom, and the weakness of God is stronger than human strength.

JESUS, Saviour of the world,
come to us in your mercy:
we look to you to save and to heal us.

By your cross and your life laid down
you set your people free:
we look to you to save and to heal us.

When they were about to perish,
you saved your disciples:
rescue us also from the brink of disaster.

In the greatness of your mercy
loose us from our chains:
forgive the sin of your people.

Make yourself known to us,
beloved Saviour and mighty Deliverer:
save us and heal us that we may praise you.

Come now and dwell with us, Christ Jesus our Saviour.
In the groaning of our prayer you are here with us.
And when all things come to be fulfilled,
may we be one with you, and share in the life of your glory.

SECOND DAY

DEAR God, you suffer the pain of creating,
even to the point of anguish and death.
In Christ you have given us our Pioneer,
that we should follow the way of your Love.

No GUILE was found on your lips, O Christ.
When reviled you did not revile in turn.
When you suffered, you did not threaten.
In the Justice of God you put your trust.

You bore our disease in your body to the tree,
that we might die to sin
and live in the ways of truth.
By your wounds we have been healed.

WE have strayed like sheep:
so let us return to the shepherd of our souls,
to the guardian of our truest selves.

O GOD, we are your servants:
you make us steady as a rock.

You have chosen us and you delight in us.
You bring your Spirit to life within us.
Through us you will make justice shine through the
world.

May we not call out like demagogues,
nor harangue from the corner of the street.
May we be too gentle to break a bruised reed,
or snuff out a flickering flame.

Never wavering, never breaking down,
let us make justice shine on every race,
planting it throughout the whole world,
as far as the coasts and the islands that wait and
yearn.

O God, you have called us to serve the cause of justice.
You have grasped us by the hand,
you have formed us and appointed us
to be a light to all peoples, a beacon to the nations.

You have called us to open eyes that are blind,
to bring prisoners out of their cells,
from the dungeons where they lie in darkness.
For you are God: to none else be the glory.

WE have been justified by faith!
We have been accepted in the Beloved!
We are at peace with you, O God of Glory!

So we exult in the hope of your splendour,
and even in the sufferings we have to endure,
as nothing compared with the glory that shall be.

For our hope is not in vain
because your love has flooded our inmost hearts
through the Holy Spirit given to us.

When we were trapped in evil ways,
you died for us, O Christ.
When we turned away our hearts,
then you proved your love for us.

And through that great love,
we are more than conquerors,
for nothing can separate us from your presence,
neither life nor death, nor angels nor powers,
nor things present nor things to come,
nor heights nor depths, nor anything in the universe.
Alleluia! Alleluia!

JESUS prayed for the soldiers,
Father forgive them for they know not what they do.
Jesus said to the penitent thief,
Today you shall be with me in Paradise.
Jesus said to his mother,
Mother – there is your son;
and to the beloved disciple he said,
Son – there is your mother.
Jesus cried out in prayer,
My God, my God, why have you forsaken me?
Jesus said,
I thirst.
Jesus said,
It is accomplished!
Jesus prayed,
Father, into your hands I commit my spirit.

WHEN I survey the wondrous cross,
   On which the Prince of Glory died,
My richest gain I count but loss,
   And pour contempt on all my pride.

Forbid it, Lord, that I should boast,
   Save in the death of Christ my God;
All the vain things that charm me most,
   I sacrifice them to his blood.

See from his head, his hands, his feet,
   Sorrow and love flow mingled down;
Did e'er such love and sorrow meet,
   Or thorns compose so rich a crown?

His dying crimson, like a robe,
   Spreads o'er his body on the tree,
Then am I dead to all the globe,
   And all the globe is dead to me.

Were the whole realm of nature mine,
   That were a present too small;
Love so amazing, so divine,
   Demands my soul, my life, my all.

THIRD DAY

My God, my God, why have you forsaken me?
Why are you so far from helping me?
O my God, I howl in the daytime,
but you do not hear me.
I groan in the watches of the night,
but I find no rest.

Yet still you are the holy God,
whom Israel has long worshipped.
Our ancestors hoped in you,
and you rescued them.
They trusted in you,
and you delivered them.
They called upon you,
and you were faithful to your covenant.
They put their trust in you
and were not disappointed.

But as for me,
I crawl the earth like a worm,
despised by others,
an outcast of the people.
All those who see me laugh me to scorn:
they make mouths at me,
shaking their heads and saying,
"He threw himself on God for deliverance:
let God rescue him then,
if God so delights in him."

You were my midwife, O God,
drawing me out of the womb.
I was weak and unknowing,
yet you were my hope,
even as I lay close to the breast,
cast upon you from the days of my birth.
From the womb of my mother
to the dread of these days
you have been my God,
never letting me go.

Do not desert me,
for trouble is hard at hand,
and there is no one to help me.
Wild beasts close in on me,
narrow-eyed, greedy and sleek.
They open their mouths and snarl at me,
like a ravening and a roaring lion.

My strength drains away like water,
and all my bones are out of joint.
My heart also in the midst of my body
is even like melting wax.
My mouth is dried up like a potsherd,
and my tongue cleaves to my gums.
My hands and my feet are withered,
you lay me down in the dust of death.

The huntsmen are all about me:
a circle of wicked men hem me in on every side,
their dogs unleashed to tear me apart.
They have pierced my hands and my feet –
I can count all my bones –
they stand staring and gloating over me.
They divide my garments among them,
they cast lots for my clothes.

The tanks of the mighty encircle me,
barbed wire and machine guns surround me.
They have marked my arm with a number,
and never call me by name.
They have stripped me of clothes and of shoes,
and showered me with gas in the chamber of death.

I cry out for morphine but no one hears me.
Pinned down by straitjacket I scream the night
    through.
I suffocate through panic in the oxygen tent.
Sweating with fear, I await news of my doom.

No one comes near with an unmasked face,
no skin touches mine in a gesture of love.
They draw back in terror, speaking only
in whispers behind doors that are sealed.

Be not far from me, O God:
you are my helper, hasten to my aid.
Deliver my very self from the sword,
my life from the falling of the axe.
Save me from the mouth of the lion,
poor body that I am, from the horns of the bull.
I will declare your name to my friends,
in the midst of the congregation I will praise you.
We stand in awe of you and bow down before you,
we glorify and magnify your name.

For you have not shrunk in loathing
from the afflicted in their suffering.
You have not hidden your face from them:
when they called to you, you heard them.

My praise is of you in the great congregation,
my vows will I perform in their sight.
We shall praise you with thanksgiving and wonder.
We shall share what we have with the poor:
they shall eat and be satisfied,
a new people, yet to be born.
Those who seek you shall be found by you:
they will be in good heart for ever.

So shall my life be preserved in your sight,
and my children shall worship you:
they shall tell of you to generations yet to come:
to a people yet to be born
they shall declare your righteousness,
that you have brought these things to fulfilment.

So let all the ends of the world remember
and turn again to their God.
Let all the families of the nations worship their Creator.

For the universe belongs to you,
and you are the Ruler of the peoples.

Can we now hold on to such faith?
Has the name of God become an offence to our
    ears?
Is God deaf to the cry of the child,
offering no relief to the burning of pain,
letting the horror of life run wild,
sitting lofty and high, refusing to act?

So do we argue and wrestle in faith,
fiercely refusing to loosen our hold.
We demand that you listen to whisper and howl,
that your deeds may fulfil your nature and name.

This is our story from Jeremiah and Job,
from all who find you obscure and perplexing.
Who are you? Who do you say that you are?
Why must we be buffeted by malice and chance?

Is our cry no more than our pride?
Is our mind too small? Is our eye too dim?
Do not quiet our pain with dazzling display.
The open wound of the child accuses you still.

Is there a cry in the depths of your being,
in the heart and soul of your chosen Christ-Self?
Stretched between earth and the heavens,
we see a striving so awesome,
a strange and harrowing love,
a bearing of pain between father and son,
a loving right through to the end,
through the worst of devil and death.

Truly you an offence, O God,
and scandalous too are the outcries of faith.
They bite deep into the lines of our faces,
as we strive to be faithful and true.
Keep us from the scandal of hypocrisy,
selfish and faithless, prayers merely mouthed,
so far from the Place of the Skull,
too indifferent to be in conflict with you,
too icily cold for your friendship.

Today if you hear the voice of *this* God,
your heart need no longer be hardened.

And can those who are buried give you worship,
those ground to the dust give you praise?
Will nothing be left but the wind and the silence,
a dead earth, abandoned, forgotten?

But you are a God who creates out of nothing,
you are a God who raises the dead,
you are a God who redeems what is lost,
you are a God who fashions new beauty,
striving with the weight of your glory,
bearing the infinite pain.

The footfalls of faith may drag through our days,
God's gift of a costly and painful enduring.
We remember your deliverance of your people of old,
we remember the abundance of the earth you have given
     us,
we remember the care and compassion of folk.
we remember your victory of long-suffering love.

The power of the powers is but a feather in the wind!
Death is transfigured to glory for ever!

EASTER

OPENING PRAYER

CHRIST is risen: alleluia, alleluia!
Christos aneste: alleluia, alleluia!

YOU have risen O Christ!
Let the gospel trumpets speak,
and the news, as of holy fire,
burning and flaming and inextinguishable,
run to the ends of the earth!

You have risen O Christ!
Let all creation greet the good news with jubilant shout,
for its redemption has come, the long night is past,
the Saviour lives, and rides and reigns in triumph
now and to the ages of ages.

Refrain at end of each line Alleluia!

IN Christ we have been reconciled to God:
Death and life have engaged each other in a wondrous
  struggle:
The Prince of Life was dead, but now lives and reigns:
We saw the tomb of the living Christ:
We saw the glory of the risen Christ:
Christ our hope is risen:
Christ is risen from the dead:

THIS is the hour of victory for our God,
the hour of God's sovereignty and power: alleluia!

All you that sleep, awake, rise from the dead,
the Light will shine upon you, Christ Jesus, alleluia!

BLESSED are you, God of love and glory:
you gave us of your very self in Jesus.
By your great mercy we have been born anew to a living
  hope
by the resurrection of Jesus Christ from the dead.

OUR Beloved Brother lives, Alleluia!
Blessedness to all he gives, Alleluia!
Laughter echoes round the earth, Alleluia!
Grief gives way to joy and mirth, Alleluia!

Hell no longer holds us fast, Alleluia!
Fate has loosed its grip at last, Alleluia!
Love has melted every fear, Alleluia!
Death proves kindly: Christ is near, Alleluia!

Celebrate this joyful feast, Alleluia!
People all, the greatest least, Alleluia!
Drop your masks of pomp and pride, Alleluia!
Greet the Clown with wounded side, Alleluia!

SUNDAY

LISTEN to me, O God, when I cry to you:
have mercy upon me and be gracious to me.
The voice of my heart has impelled me –
Seek the face of the living God.
Out of the darkness I discern your presence
in the face of the risen Christ,
revealing your pain and your joy
in new and abundant life.

Indeed you have been my helper,
you have not forgotten me, O God of my salvation.
Though my family and friends may desert me,
you will sustain me in the power of the Risen One.
Guide me in your way, O God, lead me on your path.

In the joy of your presence I can meet my adversaries,
even when false witnesses rise up against me,
or those who do me violence and wrong.

I should have utterly fainted but that I truly believe
I shall see your goodness in the land of the living.
I shall patiently wait for your good time:
I put my trust in our faithful Creator:
I shall be strong and let my heart take courage.

In all these things we are more than conquerors through Christ
who loved us. For I am sure that neither death nor life, nor angels
nor principalities nor powers, nor things present nor things to
come, nor height nor depth, nor anything else in all creation will
be able to separate us from the love of God in Christ Jesus our risen
and glorified Saviour.

Jesus said, "The hour is coming, and now is, when the dead will
hear the voice of the Son of God, and those who hear will live. For
as the Father has life in himself, so he has granted the Son also to
have life in himself, and has given him authority to execute
judgment, because he is the Son of man."

We praise you, O Christ,
risen from the dead,
breaking death's dominion,
rising from the grave.
Absorbing in yourself
the force of evil's ways,
you destroyed death's age-old sting,
and now you are alive for evermore.
Let us find our life in you,
breaking through our fear
of everlasting void.
For you are risen from the dead,
the first fruits of those who sleep.
From the days of first awareness
we betrayed the call of life,
yet yearned for that communion
which still we dimly sense.
Pain and evil, malice and cruel greed,
these deepened the sorrow of our hearts.

Yet they are done away
in light of glorious dawn,
the victory of resurrection day.
At one with all who've lived,
so all of us have died:
at one with your humanity,
all shall be made alive.

JESUS Christ is risen today, Alleluia!
Our triumphant holy day, Alleluia!
Who did once, upon the cross, Alleluia!
Suffer to redeem our loss, Alleluia!

Hymns of praise then let us sing, Alleluia!
Unto Christ, eternal King, Alleluia!
Who endured the cross and grave, Alleluia!
Sinners to redeem and save, Alleluia!

But the pains that he endured, Alleluia!
Our salvation have procured, Alleluia!
Of the universe he's King, Alleluia!
Children, men and women sing, Alleluia!

MONDAY

I LOVE you, O God my strength,
my crag, my fortress, and my deliverer,
the rock to which I cling for refuge,
my shield, my saviour and my stronghold.

I called to you with loud lamentation.
and you sprang the trap which held me fast.

The waves of death swept over my head,
the floods of chaos surged around me.
The cord of the grave tightened about my neck,
the snares of death sprang shut in my path.
In my anguish I called to you, O God:
I cried in desperation for your help.

Like an eagle you swooped down and took me,
lifting me from the jaws of the sea.
You delivered me from all that imprisoned me,
from those I thought stronger than I.
They fell upon me in the day of calamity,
yet you rescued me and led me to safety.
You brought me into a broad place,
you gave me freedom because you delight in me.

JESUS said: "I have come down from heaven, not to do my own will
but the will of him who sent me; and this is the will of him who sent
me, that I should lose nothing of all that he has given me, but raise
it up on the last day. For this is the will of my Father, that every one
who sees the Son and believes in him should have eternal life; and
I will raise him up at the last day."

THE One who walked among us,
in the Spirit obedient to the God who called,
in the sight of all created powers:
| Risen Christ, we greet you! Alleluia!

You have been proclaimed among the nations,
believed in throughout the world,
transfigured into glory:
| Risen Christ, we greet you! Alleluia!

We have set our hope on you,
the human face of God,
the Saviour of all the world:
| Risen Christ, we greet you! Alleluia!

To the Ruler of all the ages,
unseen and eternal, the only true God,
be honour and glory for ever and ever:
| Risen Christ, we greet you! Alleluia!

Good Christian folk, rejoice and sing!
Now is the triumph of our King:
To all the world glad news we bring: Alleluia!

The Lord of Life is risen for ay:
Bring flowers of song to strew his way:
Let all folk now rejoice and say: Alleluia!

Praise we in songs of victory
That Love, that Life, which cannot die,
And sing with hearts uplifted high: Alleluia!

Your name we bless, O risen Lord,
And sing today with one accord
The life laid down, the life restored: Alleluia!

TUESDAY

I deserve no reward for anything I have done,
no recompense for the cleanness of my hands.
Have I kept to your ways, O God,
and not turned aside to do evil?
Was my eye always on your command,
did I take your wisdom to heart?
I dare claim no innocence in your presence,
corrupt have been the deeds of my hands.

Yet still you delight in me – I am astonished –
loving and pursuing the one you are creating,
yearning for me to live in your image.
You are faithful even when I betray you,
when I feel the wrath of your love.
You carefully smooth out my crookedness,
forgiving my sin and wrongdoing.

Such are the faces of your love,
each reflected in the pool of my being.
For you will save a humble people,
and bring down the high looks of the proud.
You light a lamp for my path,
you make my darkness to be bright.
With your help I can meet all that comes,
with the help of my God I can face evil's defences.

God lives! God reigns!
Blessed be the rock of my salvation!
Those who set themselves against you have been
    subdued,
you have set me free from their grip,
delivering me from days of violence and
bloodshed.
For this I give you thanks among the people,
and sing praises to your name.
Great love do you show to those whom you care for,
great triumph in fulfilling your purpose of glory.

JESUS said to Martha: "I am the resurrection and the life; if you believe in me, though you die, yet shall you live, and whoever lives and believes in me shall never die. Do you believe this?" She said to him: "Yes, Lord; I believe that you are the Christ, the Son of God, he who is coming into the world."

Refrain   . . .on that last great Day.
I SHALL sing for joy and give you thanks, O God. . .
I shall trust you and have nothing to fear. . .
I shall praise you for the sternness and kindness of love. . .
I shall join my song to that of the stars. . .
For glorious in our midst shall be our faithful Creator. . .

A BRIGHTER dawn is breaking,
   And earth with praise is waking:
For thou, O King most highest,
   The power of death defiest.

O free the world from blindness,
   And fill the world with kindness,
Give sinners resurrection,
   Bring striving to perfection.

In sickness give us healing,
   In doubt thy clear revealing,
That praise to thee be given
   In earth as in thy heaven.

WEDNESDAY

TRANSGRESSION whispers to the wicked, deep in their
   hearts:
there is no fear of God in their eyes.
They flatter themselves with their own reflection,
imagining their wickedness is a secret for ever.

The words of their mouths are mischief and deceit:
they have ceased to act wisely and never do good.
They plot malice as they lie awake in the night.
They have set themselves upon a path that is crooked,
no longer aware of the evil they do.

Your steadfast love, O God, extends through the universe,
your faithfulness to the furthest stars.

Your justice is like the high mountains,
your judgment as the great deep.

So will the Judge of all the earth do right.
You will save us, frail creatures of the dust,
precious indeed is your kindness and love.

The children of earth find refuge in your shade,
you entertain them to a feast in your house,
you give them to drink from the river of delight.
For with you is the well of life;
and in your light do we see light.

Continue your goodness to those who know you,
your saving ways to the true of heart.

Let not the foot of the proud trample us,
nor the hand of the arrogant push us aside.
May those who do evil topple over and fall,
thrust down may they never rise again.

JESUS said to Mary Magdalene: "Do not hold me, for I have not yet
ascended to the Father; but go to my brethren and say to them, I
am ascending to my Father and your Father, to my God and your
God."

GREAT praise and thanks be to you, Creator God:

you have brought us through our darkness
to shine in the glory of the face of Christ;
you have brought us into the communion of saints,
to share in their heritage of light.

For Christ is the image of the invisible God,
the first-born of all creation,
in whom all things in the universe came to be,
all that we see and all that remains unseen,
all was created through Christ and for Christ.

Christ exists before creation:
in Christ all things have their being.
Christ is the Source of the Church,
the first-born from the dead, the Head of the Body.

O God, you delight that all perfection,
all completion, should be found in Christ,

and that all things in the universe
should be reconciled in Christ,
who brought peace by his life
and by his death upon the cross.

Great praise and thanks be to you, Creator God:

you have brought us through our darkness
to shine in the glory of the face of Christ;
you have brought us into the communion of saints,
to share in their heritage in light.

Lo, Jesus meets us, risen from the tomb,
  Lovingly he greets us, scatters fear and gloom;
Let the Church with gladness hymns of triumph sing,
  For her Lord now liveth, death hath lost its sting:

Thine be the glory, risen, conquering Son,
  Endless is the victory, thou o'er death hast won.

THURSDAY

IT is your royal road, O God,
it is your sovereign way –

to lead in the spirit of service,
to be stewards in your household,
to be guardians one for another,
to guide others in your paths.

As monarchs rejoice in your strength,
so may we exult in your help.

As the sovereign trusts in your faithfulness,
so do we rely on your steadfastness.

You have given us our heart's desire,
even the gift of your justice and wisdom.

You came to meet us with goodly blessings,
and placed crowns of gold on our heads.
We asked you for life and you gave it us,
long days of contentment in your presence.

You have destined even us for glory,
clothing us with splendour and honour.

You have promised us everlasting felicity,
and made us glad with the joy of your presence.

By your light we shall penetrate the dark,
striving till they yield with our enemies.

All that is evil will wither at your coming,
as the chaff is consumed in the fire.
Those who stir malice will be overwhelmed,
their plots of mischief will come to nothing.

No longer will their infection spread through the years,
to the third and the fourth generations.
You will put all their scheming to flight,
stunning them with a glance from your eye.

Be exalted, O God, in your strength,
the power of your love and your truth,
your wisdom and your justice for ever:
we shall sing for joy and praise your Name.

JESUS said to the disciples: "Thus it is written, that the Christ
should suffer and on the third day rise from the dead, and that
repentance and forgiveness of sins should be preached in his name
to all nations, beginning from Jerusalem. You are witnesses of these
things."

BLESSED are you, great God of the universe:
you gave us yourself in Jesus Christ:

in your abundant mercy we have been born anew to a
    living hope
by the resurrection of Jesus Christ from the dead.

Ours is an inheritance that nothing can destroy:
for by your power we are guarded through faith
for the coming of the full glory of your salvation.

In this we rejoice, though we suffer many trials,
trials which test the metal of our faith,
more precious than gold refined in the fire,
a faith that will then resound with praise and glory
at the revelation of Jesus Christ.

Without having seen you we love you,
we believe in you and rejoice with unutterable joy.

Alleluia, Christ is risen:
he is risen indeed, alleluia!

THIS joyful Eastertide,
Away with sin and sorrow,
My Love, the Crucified,
Hath sprung to life this morrow:

Had Christ, that once was slain,
Ne'er burst his three-day prison,
Our faith had been in vain:
But now hath Christ arisen.

FRIDAY

I WAITED patiently for you, my God,
and at last you heard my cry.
You lifted me out of the icy torrent,
you drew me out of quicksand and mire.
You set my feet on solid ground,
making firm my foothold on rock.
No longer am I empty and lost:
you have given my life new meaning.

You have put a new song in my mouth,
a song of thanksgiving and praise.
Great are the wonderful things you have done,
marvellous are your thoughts and desires.
There is none to be compared with you:
were I to declare everything you have done,
your deeds are more than I am able to express.

You have softened the wax in my ears:
I hear you at last and respond.
Open and attentive I listen to you,
I have quietened the babel of noise.

Dear God, I long to do your will.
Your law of love delights my heart.
I have not hidden your salvation in silence.
I have told of your resurrection and glory.
I have not kept back the glad news of deliverance,
your faithfulness, justice, and truth.

So may I turn and be glad in you,
so that those who love your salvation may say,

Great and wonderful is God.

Lo! I tell you a mystery. We shall not all sleep, but we shall all be
changed, in a moment, in the twinkling of an eye, at the last
trumpet call. For the trumpet will sound, and the dead will be
raised imperishable, and we shall all be changed ... When our
perishable nature puts on the imperishable, the mortal puts on
immortality, then shall come to pass the saying,
Death is swallowed up in victory.
O death, where is thy sting?
O grave, where is thy victory?

BLESSED are you, O God, who chose us in Christ
before the foundation of the world,
that we should be whole and holy before you.

You destined us in love
to be your daughters and sons in Christ,
according to the purpose of your will,
to the praise of your glorious grace
freely lavished on us in the Beloved.

In Christ we have redemption through his blood,
the forgiveness of our sins,
according to the riches of your grace.

For you have made known to us the mystery of your will,
your purpose to unite all things in Christ,
in the heavens and on the earth,
so that all may resound to your glory.

> LOVE's redeeming work is done,
>   Fought the fight, the battle won:
> Lo! our Sun's eclipse is o'er!
>   Lo! he sets in blood no more!
>
> Vain the stone, the watch, the seal,
>   Christ has burst the gates of hell;
> Death in vain forbids his rise;
>   Christ has opened Paradise.

SATURDAY

GOD is my light and my salvation:
whom then shall I fear?
God is the strength of my life:
of whom then shall I be afraid?
In God alone do I put my trust:
how then can others harm me?

I have desired of God one thing,
and still I eagerly desire it,
that I may dwell in the house of my God
all the days of my life,
to feast my eyes on the beauty of my Creator,
to ponder deeply the gracious will of my God.

In the time of my trouble
you will hide me in your shelter;
in the shadow of your tent
you will conceal me
from those who pursue me;
high on a pinnacle of rock
you will place me safe
from those who surge around me.

Therefore I will offer in your dwelling place
gifts with great gladness;
I will sing and praise your name.

JESUS said: "I will not leave you desolate; I will come to you. Yet a
little while, and the world will see me no more, but you will see me;
because I live, you will live also. In that day you will know that I am
in my Father, and you in me, and I in you."

MEN and women: praise the God of Love!
Earth and sky: worship the Creator!
Angels, heavenly powers, cherubim and seraphim,
raise the everlasting shout:
Holy, holy, holy, great God of power and love,
the whole creation is full of your glory.
Glorious company of apostles: alleluia!
Honoured fellowship of prophets: alleluia!
White-robed gathering of martyrs: alleluia!
Communion of saints in all times and places
proclaim the glorious Name:
Giver of life, of splendour and wonder!
Bearer of pain, graceful and true!
Maker of love, flaming and passionate!

Christ, we greet you in your glory,
hidden deep in the being of God,
Word made flesh to deliver us,
glad to be born of Mary,
destroying the sting of death,
opening the road to the presence of God,
guarding the freedom of the creation,
yearning for the gathering of the harvest.
Come, then, judge and deliver us,
who are freed at the cost of your life,
and lead us with all your saints
to lands of eternal glory.

JESUS lives! thy terrors now
  Can, O Death, no more appal us;
Jesus lives! by this we know
  Thou, O grave, canst not enthral us: Alleluia.

Jesus lives! henceforth is death
  But the gate of life immortal;
This shall calm our trembling breath
  When we pass its gloomy portal: Alleluia.

Jesus lives! our hearts know well
  Nought from us his love shall sever;
Life, nor death, nor powers of hell
  Tear us from his keeping ever: Alleluia.

PRAYER FOR EACH DAY

O GOD of Light and Life, of Love ever-renewed,
proclaiming Yes to all that Jesus is
and all that he said and did and suffered,
we give you praise and glory,
for you burst the gates of hell,
you destroy sin and death,
you render the powers helpless to harm,
you give your people eternal life,
you bring all humanity from death to life,
you gladden our hearts,
you give us joy.

RISEN Christ, come in your victorious power,
affirm in us the goodness of God,
give us new life,
reconcile us in peace,
strengthen us in the assurance of final triumph,
make us faithful in witness,
fulfil in us your promises.

O CHRIST, radiant Light, shining in our darkness,
most glorious of the children of earth,
Holy One setting captives free:
I Alleluia!

O Christ, stooping low in great humility,
obedient to death, walking the way of the cross,
calling us to follow to death and to resurrection:
I Alleluia!

O Christ, saving us in our poverty,
reconciling us to the Source of all that is,
making us a holy people, a commonwealth,
and priests to our God:
I Alleluia!

O Christ, granting us the fulness of your grace,
saving us from death,
giving us a share in your life:
I Alleluia!

O Christ, burning in us all that is not kindled by your
presence,
melting in us all that freezes and keeps us cold:
I Alleluia!

ASCENSION

OPENING PRAYER

THE pioneer of our salvation
has triumphed over suffering and death.
The firstborn among many brothers and sisters
has led the way into the presence of God.

LET our bearing towards one another
flow out of our life in you, O Christ.
You shared the nature of God,
but did not cling to God's power.
You lived among us as a slave,
humble and obedient.
You accepted all that came,
even a criminal's death.
So God has lifted you high,
and given you the greatest of names,
that at the name of Jesus
the living and the dead
should greet you as their Saviour,
to the glory and praise of God.

ODD-NUMBERED DAYS

CREATOR God, Source of all life,
how gloriously does your name resound,
echoing to the bounds of the universe!

The morning stars sing for joy,
and the youngest child cries your name.
So the weak in the world shame the strong,
and silence the proud and rebellious.

When I look at the heavens,
even the work of your fingers,
the moon and the stars
majestic in their courses,

the eagle riding the air,
the dolphin ploughing the sea,
the gazelle leaping the wind,
the sheep grazing the fells,

who are we human beings
that you keep us in mind,
children, women and men,
that you care so much for us?

Yet still you bring us to life,
creating us after your image,
stewards of the planet
you give as our home.

How awesome a task
you entrust to our hands,
how fragile and beautiful
is the good earth!

Creator God, Source of all life,
how gloriously does your name resound,
echoing to the bounds of the universe!

O saviour God, you have set us free:
We will trust you and not be afraid.
You are our strength and our song:
you have become our salvation.
With joy we shall draw living water
from the deep wells of your redeeming love.

We thank you, O God, and call upon your name.
We shall make your deeds known among the nations,
we shall proclaim your glorious name: Alleluia!

You have triumphed gloriously:
let it be known all over the earth.
Let us shout and sing for joy.
Great in our midst is the beloved and holy God.

Glory and honour and praise
are yours by right, O God our Maker.
For you are creating all things,
and by your will they have their being.

Glory and honour and praise
are yours by right, O Lamb who was slain,
for by your lifeblood you rescued us from slavery,
and brought us into the presence of God.

Folk of every race and language,
you have made us a priestly people,
to stand in your presence and serve you.
Praise and honour, glory and love
be given to the One who reigns and to the Lamb.

You have raised our human nature
  In the clouds to God's fair land;
There we feast in heavenly places,
  There with you in glory stand;
Jesus reigns, adored by angels;
  Seeds bear fruit that once were sown:
Love that died, in your ascension
  We by faith behold our own.

EVEN-NUMBERED DAYS

DEAR God, you are creating the earth
and all that is in it,
the whole round world
and all who dwell on land or sea.
You have founded life upon the waters,
and drawn it forth from the mysterious deeps.

Who shall climb the mountain of God?
Who shall stand in the holy place?
Those who have clean hands and pure hearts,
who have not set their minds on falsehood,
nor sworn to deceive their neighbours.
They shall receive a blessing from God,
and justice from the God of their salvation.
Such is the fortune of those who draw near their
    Creator,
who seek the face of the God of Jacob.

Let the gates be opened,
let the doors be lifted high,
that the great procession may come in.
| Who is the One clothed with glory?
It is our God, the God who has triumphed,
who has striven with evil and prevailed.

Let the gates be opened,
let the doors be lifted high,
that the great procession may come in.
Who is the One clothed with glory?
It is the great God of all the universe,
glorious in a Love that never fails.

O LIGHT of Light,
God of shining splendour,
your glory is rising upon us,
brighter than a million suns.

Even though night still covers the earth,
and thick darkness the peoples,
your glory is rising upon us,
your dawn gives light to the sky.

The whole world will come to your Light,
the powerful to the brightness of your dawning.
The gates of the city will be flung open,
never to be closed, by day or by night.

The years of our wounding will be over,
the eyes of malice and greed will vanish,
the look of terror and grief turn to joy.

City of God, City of all peoples,
the sound of violence will be heard no more in your
    streets,
no longer the looting and crackle of flames.

You will call your walls Salvation,
and your gates will be named Peace.

No more will the sun give you daylight,
nor the light of the moon shine upon you.
But your God will be your splendour,
your glory, and your own lasting light.

SALVATION and glory and power belong to you, O God:
your judgments are true and just.
We your servants give you praise,
for we hold you in awe, both small and great.
You reign in glory, O God,
let us rejoice and give you praise.
The marriage of the Lamb has come,
bride and bridegroom are ready.
Praise and honour, glory and love be to the Lamb,
the One who was slain from before the world was made,
who shares the reign of God: Alleluia, alleluia!

O HOW glorious and resplendent
    Fragile body shalt thou be,
When endued with so much beauty,
    Full of life and strong and free,
Full of vigour, full of pleasure,
    That shall last eternally!

PRAYERS FOR EACH DAY

WE give you thanks, O God,
that Christ is our High Priest,
living your life of sacrificial love,
continually presenting the offering of himself.
Of your abundant grace,
give us what we need
to follow in the narrow way of sacrifice,
that we may attain to the stature of the fulness of Christ,
and be Christ's body in the world.

We praise you that Christ indeed reigns in glory,
and we pray that at the name of Jesus
every knee shall bow and every voice shout wonder.

We bless you that we have been raised with Christ
to new and eternal life,
and we pray that you will give us grace
to seek those things that endure,
and that the peace of Christ may reign in our hearts.

We thank you that the needs and agonies of humankind
are borne deep in the wounds of Christ,
into the pain-bearing love of God,
and we pray for all who are enduring pain,
that they may put their trust in you.

We rejoice that all who are alive
and all who have departed this life
will, in the glory and peace of Christ,
share unimaginable riches of your grace
when, in the fulness of time,
all things in the universe are united and made whole.

PENTECOST

OPENING PRAYER

SEND forth, O God, your Spirit,
and renew the face of the earth.
Come, Creator Spirit,
fill the hearts of your people.
Water, wind, and flame, come:
cleanse us, enliven us, set us on fire
with love for our God: alleluia, alleluia!

PSALMS

BLESSED be you, O God our Creator:
you teach our hands to shape chaos,
our fingers to strive with intractable clay.
You are the source of our power and our skill,
Creator Spirit rising deep from within.

Who are we that you should keep us in mind,
children of earth that you should care for us?
We are but a breath of wind,
our days like a shadow that passes away.

You could dazzle us with displays of great power,
touching the mountains so that they smoke,
darting forth your lightnings,
scattering them on every side,
loosing missiles with the hiss of flame.

Yet you strove with evil and destroying power,
not with the matching of strength,
but absorbing the hurt in your dying,
winning through to a new kind of life.

In that Spirit be with us in chaos and fear,
when the waters foam and rage,
that we may pierce to the eye of the storm,
and know the sustaining love of your presence.

Then we shall sing a new song,
on flute and harp singing your praise.
We shall be blessed and delight in your ways,
and give you the praise, O God our God.

DEAR God, are you the Friend I can trust?
You seem so deaf to my prayer,
to the urgent sound of my voice.
Do you not hear, do you turn away silent,
when I cry out for help?
I lift up my hands in the holy place,
but still I hear no answer.

Let me pause and remember
the holy ground of your presence –
the bush burning with light
at the moment of despair.

You are here in the ones I ignore,
the shuffling old man in the street,
the hollow-eyed woman unkempt,
the neighbour I pass hurriedly by.

I see neither their need nor mine,
it is I who turn silent away.
I collude with the ways of wickedness,
speaking peace with my lips,
unaware of the mischief of my heart.
No wonder I do not hear your voice:
I turn away from your presence,
pulled down by my selfish desires.

Open our eyes that we may see,
unblock our ears that we may hear.
Send us the fury of the desert wind,
or the gentle breeze through the trees.
Whether by shouting or whisper,
face us with dark truths of our ways.

No reward dare we claim,
no generosity from your heart.
No wonder we fall in the midst of our devices,
to be built up in strength no more.

And yet there are times of our passion,
our anger at the traps of the poor,
of those without power or numbers.
The voice of the voiceless is heard in our land,
and the sound of your rejoicing, O God.
You are the strength of our hands
as we strive with the powers for your truth.
Our hearts trust you and we thank you,
we dance for joy and with songs give you praise.

READINGS

JESUS said: "Truly, truly I say to you, unless you are born of water
and the Spirit, you cannot enter the kingdom of God. That which
is born of the flesh is flesh, and that which is born of the Spirit is
spirit. Do no marvel that I said to you, 'You must be born anew.'
The wind blows where it wills, and you hear the sound of it, but
you do not know whence it comes or whither it goes; so it is with
every one who is born of the Spirit."

Jesus said to the woman of Samaria: "Every one who drinks of the
water from this well will thirst again, but if you drink of the water
that I shall give you, you will never thirst; the water that I shall give
you will become in you a spring of water welling up to eternal life."

I will pour clean water upon you, and cleanse you from every taint
of ill.
I will give you a new heart and put a new spirit within you.
I will take the heart of stone from your body, and give you a heart
of flesh.
I will put my spirit within you, and you shall live by my law.
You shall become my people, and I will be your God.

PRAYER AND HYMN

Come, O wind, from every quarter of the earth,
breathe into these dry bones that they may live.
Let sinews and flesh come upon them,
and breathe the wind of your spirit into them,
and we shall know that you are God.

> Come holy flame and burn
> Till earthly passions turn
>   To gold and silver
>   In your heat refining.
> And let your glorious light
> Shine ever on my sight,
>   And clothe me round,
>   The while my path illuming.

TRINITY

OPENING PRAYER

GREAT praise and everlasting glory be to God,
Father, Son, and Holy Spirit,
Creator, Redeemer, Sanctifier,
Lover, Beloved, and the Love between,
Giver of life, Bearer of pain, Maker of love,
Alpha and Omega, the beginning and the end.
Great praise and everlasting glory be to God,
at all times, in all places,
through the centuries, throughout the universe.
Holy, holy, holy, great God of power and love,
who was and who is and who is to come.

PSALM

DEAR God, you have been our refuge
from one generation to another.
Before the mountains rose from the sea,
or ever the earth and the world were formed,
you are eternal, world without end.

You change us back to the dust saying,
Return, O children of earth.
A thousand years in your sight are but as yesterday,
even as it were a day that is past.
As a watch in the night comes quickly to an end,
so the years pass before your eyes.

They are even like the grass,
which in the morning is green,
but by the evening is dried up and withered.
We consume away in your fire,
we are afraid at the burning of the dross.
You have laid bare our misdeeds before us,
our secret sins in the light of your countenance.

The years of our days are threescore and ten,
perhaps even to eighty for those who are strong.
Yet is their span but labour and sorrow,
so soon do they pass away and we are gone.

But who is attentive to the purging of your wrath,
or who considers the fierceness of your love?

So teach us to number our days,
and apply our hearts to wisdom.
Turn again, O God, do not delay:
be gracious to your servants.
Satisfy us in the morning
with your loving kindness.
So shall we rejoice and be glad
all the days of our life.

READING

BLESSED be you, O God, the God and Father of our Lord Jesus
Christ; you have blessed us in Christ with every spiritual blessing
in the heavenly places...
You destined us in love to be your sons and daughters through
Jesus Christ, according to the purpose of your will, to the praise of
your glorious grace, which you have freely bestowed on us in the
Beloved...
In Christ we also, who have heard the word of truth, the gospel of
our salvation, and have believed in Christ, were sealed with your
promised Holy Spirit, which is the guarantee of our inheritance
until we acquire possession of it, to the praise of your glory...

PRAYER

O GOD, we give you thanks
because you have revealed your glory
as the glory of your Son and of the Holy Spirit,
three persons equal in glory,
undivided in splendour,
yet one Creator, one God,
ever to be worshipped and adored.

CANTICLE

WE give you glory, Giver of life,
and great thanksgiving, Bearer of pain;
to the Maker of love, unending praise!

Voices of countless angels praise you,
myriads upon myriads, thousands upon thousands,
sing to you without ceasing:
Alleluia, alleluia!

Holy, holy, holy is God, the sovereign Ruler of all,
who was and who is and who is to come:
Alleluia, alleluia!

Victory and power and glory belong to you, O God:
true and just are your judgments:
Alleluia! Alleluia!

All your servants praise you, O God,
those who look to you in love and awe:
Alleluia, alleluia!

Our God, our faithful Creator, reigns:
let us exult and shout for joy and give you glory:
Alleluia, alleluia!

We give you glory, Giver of life,
and great thanksgiving, Bearer of pain;
to the Maker of love, unending praise!

HYMNS

HOLY, Holy, Holy! Living Flame of Glory!
Early in the morning our song shall rise to thee.
Holy, Holy, Holy! Strong in love and mercy!
God in three Persons, Blessed Trinity!

Holy, Holy, Holy! All the saints adore thee,
Casting down their golden crowns around the glassy
sea.
Cherubim and seraphim falling down before thee,
God of all time and all eternity.

Holy, Holy, Holy! Though the darkness hide thee,
  Though our eye through human sin thy glory may not see,
Only thou art holy, there is none beside thee,
  Perfect in power, in love, and purity.

Holy, Holy, Holy! Beating Heart of Glory!
  All thy works shall praise thy name, in earth and sky and
    sea.
Holy, Holy, Holy! Strong in love and mercy!
  God in three Persons, Blessed Trinity!

I BIND unto myself today
  The strong name of the Trinity,
By invocation of the same,
  The Three in One and One in Three.

I bind this day to me for ever
  By power of faith Christ's Incarnation;
His baptism in Jordan river,
  His death on Cross for my salvation;
His bursting from the spicèd tomb,
  His riding up the heavenly way;
His coming at the day of doom;
  I bind unto myself today.

I bind unto myself today
  The power of God to hold and lead,
His eye to watch, his might to stay,
  His ear to hearken to my need.
The wisdom of my God to teach,
  His hand to guide, his shield to ward;
The word of God to give me speech,
  His heavenly host to be my guard.

I bind unto myself today
   The virtues of the star-lit heaven,
The glorious sun's life-giving ray,
   The whiteness of the moon at even,
The flashing of the lightning free,
   The whirling wind's tempestuous shocks,
The stable earth, the deep salt sea,
   Around the old eternal rocks.

I bind unto myself the name,
   The strong name of the Trinity;
By invocation of the same,
   The Three in One, and One in Three.
Of whom all nature hath creation;
   Eternal Father, Spirit, Word:
Praise to the God of my salvation,
   Salvation is of Christ the Lord.

CREATION

PRELUDE

IN the beginning God created the heavens and the earth.
The earth was without form and void,
and darkness was upon the face of the deep.
And the Spirit of God was moving over the face of the
 waters.

IN the beginning was the Word,
and the Word was with God and the Word was God,
through whom all things came to be,
without whom was not anything made that was made.

PSALM

LET all the powers of the universe praise the Creator,
ascribe to God glory and strength.
In the beauty of holiness we worship you, O God,
giving you the honour due to your name.

Your voice rolls over the waters,
your glory thunders over the oceans.
Your voice resounds through the mountains,
echoing glory and splendour.

Your voice splits even the cedar trees,
breaking in pieces the cedars of Lebanon.
The trees of the mountainside howl in your wind,
uprooted like matchsticks in the roar of your passing.

Your voice divides the lightning flash,
flames of fire come from your tongue.
Your voice whirls the sands of the desert,
the whistling sands of the desert storm.

Your voice makes the oaks shake and shudder,
and strips the forest bare,
and all in your presence cry, Glory!

O God, more powerful than tempest and flood,
reigning over all your creation,
stillness in the eye of the storm,
give strength to your people in awe of you,
give your people the blessing of peace.

BENEDICITE

LET all created beings bless you, O God,
sing your praise and exalt you for ever.
May the heavens bless you, O God,
sing your praise and exalt you for ever.

Let your angels bless you, O God,
your archangels sing your praise.
May the cherubim and seraphim bless you, O God,
sing your praise and exalt you for ever.

Let sun and moon bless you, O God,
the stars of night sing your praise.
May rain and dew bless you, O God,
sing your praise and exalt you for ever.

Let the winds that blow bless you, O God,
fire and heat sing your praise.
May scorching wind and bitter cold bless you, O God,
sing your praise and exalt you for ever.

Let sunset and dawn bless you, O God,
the nights and days sing your praise.
May light and darkness bless you, O God,
sing your praise and exalt you for ever.

Let frost and cold bless you, O God,
ice and snow sing your praise.
May lightning and thunder bless you, O God,
sing your praise and exalt you for ever.

Let the earth bless you, O God,
mountains and valleys sing your praise.
May all that grows in the ground bless you, O God,
sing your praise and exalt you for ever.

Let springs of water bless you, O God,
seas and rivers sing your praise.
May whales and all that swim in the waters bless you,
    O God,
sing your praise and exalt you for ever.

Let the birds of the air bless you, O God,
beasts and cattle sing your praise.
May all folk who dwell on the face of the earth bless you,
    O God,
sing your praise and exalt you for ever.

Let your people bless you, O God,
your ministers sing your praise.
May your servants bless you, O God,
sing your praise and exalt you for ever.

Let all folk of upright spirit bless you, O God,
the holy and humble of heart sing your praise.
May we bless the Trinity of Love,
sing your praise and exalt you for ever.

READING

I CONSIDER that the sufferings of this present time are not worth comparing with the glory that is to be revealed to us. For the creation waits with eager longing for the revealing of the children of God; for the creation was subjected to futility, not of its own will but by the will of him who subjected it in hope; because the creation itself will be set free from its bondage to decay and obtain the glorious liberty of the children of God.

CANTICLE OF THE SUN

MOST High, Omnipotent, Good Lord,
praise, glory, and honour be given to you with one accord.
To you alone, Most High, does praise belong,
yet none is worthy to make of you her song.

Be praised my God with all your works whate'er they be,
our noble Brother Sun especially,
whose brightness makes the light by which we see,
and he is fair and radiant, splendid and free,
a likeness of your glory that we have yet to see.

Be praised my God for Sister Moon and every Star
that you have formed to shine so clear from heaven afar.

Be praised my God for Brother Wind and Air,
breezes and clouds and weather foul or fair –
to every one that breathes you give a share.

Be praised my God for Sister Water, sure,
none is so useful, humble, or so pure.

Be praised my God for Brother Fire, whose light
you have given to illuminate the night,
and he is fair and merry and strong and bright.

Be praised my God for Sister Earth our Mother,
who nourishes and gives us food and fodder,
and the green grass and flowers of every colour.

Be praised my God for those who for your love forgive,
contented unavenged in quiet to live.
Blessed those who in the way of peace are found –
by you O God Most High they shall be crowned.

Be praised my God for our Sister Bodily Death,
from whom none can escape that has drawn breath.
Woe to those whom life and love do kill,
blessed those who find that in your holy will
the second Death to them will bring no ill.

Praise and bless our God, and give your service due,
with humblest thanks for all that God has given you.

HYMN

O PRAISE ye the Lord!
   Praise him in the height,
Rejoice in his word,
   Ye angels of light;
Ye heavens, adore him,
   By whom ye were made,
And worship before him,
   In brightness arrayed.

O praise ye the Lord!
   Thanksgiving and song
To him be outpoured
   All ages along;
For love in creation,
   For heaven restored,
For grace of salvation,
   O praise ye the Lord!

SAINTS' DAYS

OPENING PRAYER

DEAR God, you love us
and have freed us from our sins
in the lifeblood of Christ:
to you be glory and praise for ever!

If we die with you, we shall live with you;
if we endure, we shall reign with you, alleluia!
If we share your suffering now,
we shall share your splendour hereafter, alleluia!

PSALM

DEAR God, who are the honoured guests in your tent?
Who may dwell in your presence upon your holy
    mountain?
Who may commune with those who are your heart's
    desire,
lovingly embraced in the union of friends?

Those who lead uncorrupt lives,
and do the thing that is right,
who speak the truth from their hearts,
and have not slandered with their tongue.

Those who have not betrayed their friends,
nor rained down abuse on their neighbours,
in whose eyes the shifty have no honour,
but hold in high esteem those who fear God.

Those who give their word to their neighbour,
and do not go back on their promise,
who have not grown wealthy at the expense of the poor,
or grown sleek with flattery and bribes.

Those who recognize the outcast as the one whom they
    need,
who forgive to seventy times seven,
who depend on the mercy of God,
and live their lives by the law of love.

Those who are steadfast and kind,
who are resilient and patient and humble,
who know the cost of a morsel of justice,
a glimpse of compassion in times that are savage.

Their roots are deep in the being of God,
their arms are spread wide in welcome embrace.
They are faithful, joyful, and blessed,
God's sisters and brothers and friends.

READING

SINCE we are surrounded by so great a cloud of witnesses, let us also
lay aside every weight, and sin which clings so closely, and let us
run with perseverance the race that is set before us, looking to Jesus
the pioneer and perfecter of our faith, who for the joy that was set
before him endured the cross, despising the shame, and is seated
at the right hand of the throne of God.

CANTICLE

O LAMB you have conquered and reign!
And your victory will be shared by your followers,
called and chosen and faithful, alleluia!

These are the words of the First and the Last,
who was dead and came to life again:

To the one who is victorious
I will give the right to eat from the Tree of Life
that stands in the Garden of God: alleluia!
Be faithful to death,
and I will give you the crown of life: alleluia!

To the one who is victorious
I will give some of the hidden manna,
and I will give also a white stone: alleluia!
And on the stone will be written a new name,
known only to the one who receives it: alleluia!

To the one who is victorious,
who perseveres in doing my will to the end,
I will give authority over the nations, alleluia!
the same authority that I received from the Eternal;
and I will give also the star of dawn: alleluia!

The one who is victorious
shall be made a pillar in the temple of God
and shall never leave it, alleluia!
upon whom I will write the name of my God
and the name of the City of my God,
and my own new name, alleluia!

To the one who is victorious
I will give a place in my company,
as I myself was victorious, alleluia!
and now dwell in the presence of the Eternal, alleluia!

These are the words of the Amen,
the faithful and true witness.

O Lamb you have conquered and reign!
And your victory will be shared by your followers,
called and chosen and faithful, alleluia!

PRAYER

Refrain   . . .to God be the glory:
           I Thanks be to God for ever.

For Abraham and Sarah, ancestors of the faithful, journeying to
an unknown future, trusting the promise. . .

For Jacob, deceiving younger brother, yet chosen by God, ancestor
of those called by no virtue of their own. . .

For Moses, who led the people of Israel to freedom and a new
land. . .

For the Prophets who spoke the truth whatever the cost. . .

For Ruth, whose loyalties transcended land and family. . .

For Mary, mother of the Lord, and all who, like her, have trusted and obeyed...

For the first disciples who left all to follow Jesus...

For the women who followed Jesus and did not desert him, first witnesses of the Resurrection...

For the apostles who preached the Gospel and healed the sick...

For the writers of the Gospels, and for those who have brought the faith of Christ alive for each generation...

For the unknown Chione of Anatolia, whose epitaph affirmed she had found Jerusalem for she had prayed much...

For the great company of martyrs who faced death for love of Christ and in his strength...

For missionaries of every race who have shared the love of God with men and women different from themselves...

For those who brought the Gospel to our own land and nourished the life of the Church, for Patrick and David, for Augustine and Dunstan, for Cuthbert and Aidan, for Bede and Hilda...

For those who have reformed the Church of God and for those who have held firm to its continuing faith...

For those who have sought to transform the world in the light of the Spirit of Christ...

For those who have led hidden lives of faithful prayer and quiet service...

For God's witnesses in our own century, for its many martyrs and for its peacemakers...

For all the unsung saints whose names are forgotten but whose influence lives on...

For those in our own lives who have brought us to this time and place...

Let us praise them with great praise
I and give thanks for them to God:
Blessing and honour and glory and love
I be to our God for ever and ever. Amen.

HYMN

FOR all the saints who from their labours rest,
Who in the world their faith in God confessed,
Your name, O Jesus, be for ever blessed: Alleluia!

You were the Stranger in the dark of night
With whom they strove to find their one true light,
To whom you gave God's blessing ever bright: Alleluia!

They are the folk who gave with love divine,
Always in service did their wills incline,
Forgetting self, they did with glory shine: Alleluia!

They followed you, cast out the city's gate,
Killed by the eyes and guns of human hate,
Yet trumpets sound their resurrection fête: Alleluia!

And there will dawn a yet more glorious day,
The saints with laughter sing and dance and play,
The Clown of glory tumbles in the Way: Alleluia!

With earth restored, with this our fragile star,
In gladness home from pilgrimage afar,
We find in God a joy that none can mar: Alleluia!

THE DEPARTED

KONTAKION FOR THE DEPARTED

GIVE rest O Christ to your servant with your saints,
where sorrow and pain are no more,
neither sighing, but life everlasting.
Creator and Maker of humankind, you only are
    immortal,
and we are mortal, formed of the earth,
and to the earth we shall return:
for so you did ordain when you created us, saying,
Dust thou art and unto dust thou shalt return.
All we go down to the dust,
and, weeping o'er the grave, we make our song:
Alleluia, alleluia, alleluia.
Give rest O Christ to your servant with your saints,
where sorrow and pain are no more,
neither sighing, but life everlasting.

PSALM

O GOD our refuge and strength,
preserve us from lasting harm.
Again and again we affirm,
in times of doubt and of trust,
You are our faithful Creator,
in you alone is our bliss.

We thank you for all your holy people,
all whose lives give you glory.
We praise you for your martyrs and saints,
in whom you take great delight.

As for those held in high esteem,
those idols adored by the crowd,
those gods they fête and run after,
we will not take their name on our lips.
They are bloated with pride and success,
punctured by thorns in the late autumn wind.

Your name alone do we praise,
our resting place now and for ever.
You feed us with the Bread of Life,
you nourish us with the Cup of Salvation.

We have been so fortunate in our days,
and in the places where we have lived.
To no one else belongs the praise
but to you, the great Giver of gifts.

We give you thanks for the wisdom of your counsel,
even at night you have instructed our hearts.
In the silence of the darkest of hours
we open our ears to the whisper of your voice.

We have set your face always before us,
in every cell of our being you are there.
As we tremble on the narrowest of paths,
the steadying of your hand gives us courage.
Fleet of foot, with our eyes on the goal,
headlong in the chasm we shall not fall.

Therefore our hearts rejoice and our spirits are glad,
our whole being shall rest secure.
For you will not give us over to the power of Death,
nor let your faithful ones see the Pit.

You will show us the path of life;
in your countenance is the fulness of joy.
From the spring of your heart flow rivers of delight,
a fountain of water that shall never run dry.

READING

I SAW in my mind's eye a vision:
a new realm, a new order, a new earth,
for the old had decayed and passed away.
Even the seas of chaos had been calmed.
And I saw the holy city, new Jerusalem,
coming out of the clouds of God's presence,
prepared as a bride and a bridegroom
are adorned as gifts to each other.
And I heard the voice of the One who reigns:
Behold, I come to dwell among you, my people,
and you will live in my presence.

I will wipe away every tear from your eyes,
and death shall be no more,
neither shall there be mourning,
nor crying, nor pain, any more.
The former things have passed away:
I make all things new.

PRAYERS

WE give you thanks, O God, because through Christ you have given us the hope of a glorious resurrection, so that although death comes to us all, yet we rejoice in the promise of eternal life; for to your faithful people life is changed, not taken away, and when our mortal flesh is laid aside, an everlasting dwelling place is made ready for us in heaven.

O God of the living, in whose embrace all peoples live, in whatever world or condition they may be, we send our love in prayer to those whose names and needs and dwelling place are known to you, giving you thanks for our memories of them. Tell them, O loving God, how much we love them, and as we greet them across the tender bridge in Christ, may this our prayer minister to their growing and their peace.

A GREETING IN LOVE

THE God of peace sanctify you completely,
even to the glory of the great day:
faithful is the God who calls,
the God whose promises will be fulfilled.

N,
God bless you richly,
grow in grace,
make love,
keep me in loving mind,
hold me close in the Presence,
guide me,
pray for me.

AN ACT OF REMEMBRANCE

LET us remember those citizens of this country and of the commonwealth, especially those from this city (town, village) and from our own families, who gave their lives in the world wars, those who survived, but wounded to the end of their days, in heart or mind or body, and those who were bereaved and who have never since found so close a love . . .

Let us remember those who died in the bombing of the cities, of Coventry and Dresden, of London and Hiroshima . . .

Let us remember those who have died in wars since, in South-East Asia, in the Middle East, in Africa, in Northern Ireland, in the South Atlantic . . .

Let us remember those who have died through acts of terrorism, blown out of the skies or gunned down in the streets of the world's cities . . .

Let us remember all who have died as a result of our individual and corporate pride and greed, our folly and despair . . .

Let us remember the groaning of the whole creation, of animals slaughtered for profit or amusement, of the forests, soil, and waters of the good earth, raped by the unheeding . . .

Let us remember those who have suffered at the hands of ruthless men and women who would commit genocide, especially the fanatics who pursue a so-called holy war and claim the will of God...

Let us remember those who have died, and continue to do so, in dark cells and concentration camps, prisoners of conscience, witnesses to faith, courageous prophets who disturb the powers that be...

Let us remember our Jewish brothers and sisters whom Christians have treated so ill for so long; let us remember their Six Million who died in the Holocaust in Germany and Poland, and those others who died with them, Jehovah's Witnesses, homosexual people, gypsies, all whose way of life challenged the claim of the purity of the race...

Let us remember with penitence the seeds of murder within each one of us...

So we remember those who sanctified God's name on earth and those who died out of duty and for their friends...

So we remember those who died when madness ruled the world, and evil dwelt on earth, those we knew and those whose very name is lost. Because of their sacrifice, may we renew our fight against cruelty and injustice, against prejudice, tyranny, and oppression. Still we cry to God out of the darkness of our divided world. Let not the hope of men and women perish. Let not new clouds rain death upon the earth. Turn to yourself the hearts and wills of rulers and peoples, that a new world may arise where men and women live as friends in the bond of your peace.

HYMN OF DEDICATION

I vow to you, my friends of earth,
    all worldly things above,
Entire and whole – yet broken –
    the service of my love:
The love that dares to question,
    the love that speaks its name,
That flowers still in barren ground,
    yet hides no more for shame;
The love that struggles through the pain,
    and whispers in the night,
Yet shares its secret with the world,
    to bring the truth to light.

This *is* that other country
    we heard of long ago,
When called to be the spies of God
    where milk and honey flow:
A world where hurts find healing,
    where all th'oppressed run free,
Where friends who have been sore betrayed
    each other truly see:
It is our earth, transfigured, new,
    where wars and hatreds cease,
Where spy and friend walk hand in hand
    in Christ our Lover's Peace.

ORDINARY DAYS

OPENING PSALM FOR EACH DAY

LET us sing to the God who is creating us,
let us rejoice in the Rock of our salvation.

Dear God, we celebrate your presence with thanksgiving,
and with our whole heart sing psalms of praise.
We greet you with love, Creator of the universe,
Spirit who strives with the chaos of the world.
With your finger you shape the mountains of the earth,
and the depths of the valleys are scoured by your power.
The wings of your Spirit brood over the seas,
and your hands mould the dry land.

O come let us worship and lift our hearts high,
and adore our God, our Creator.

For you indeed are God, and we are your people,
crafted by the skill of your hands.

OR

LET the whole earth be joyful in you, O God,
serve you with gladness,
and celebrate your presence with a song.

For we know that you are creating us,
you have made us and we belong to you.
We are your people, and the sheep of your pasture.

We find our way into your gates with thanksgiving,
and into your house with praise.
We give you thanks and bless your holy name.

For you are gracious, your mercy is everlasting,
your faithfulness endures from generation to generation.

[*After the psalm and reading for the day, turn to p. 162ff for the Canticles and then to p. 166ff for the Concluding Prayers.*]

DAY 1: PSALM AND READING

WOE to us when we walk in the ways of wickedness,
when we bend our ear to the counsel of deceit,
and scoff at what is holy from the seat of pride.

Blessings upon us when we delight in the truth of God,
and ponder God's Law by day and by night,
when we stand up for truth in face of the lie,
when we mouth no slogans and betray no friends.

Then we shall grow like trees
planted by streams of water,
that yield their fruit in due season,
whose leaves do not wither.

We struggle with evil in our hearts,
tossed to and fro like chaff in the wind,
a rootless people whose lives have no meaning,
unable to stand when judgment comes,
desolate, outside the house of our God.

May ways of wickedness perish among us:
forgive us, O God, and renew us,
lead us in paths of justice and truth,
obedient to your wisdom and will,
trusting in the hope of your promise.

JOHN looked at Jesus as he walked, and said, "Behold, the Lamb
of God!" The two disciples heard him say this, and they followed
Jesus. Jesus turned, and saw them following, and said to them,
"What do you seek?" And they said to him, "Rabbi" (which
means Teacher), "where are you dwelling?" He said to them,
"Come and see."

DAY 2: PSALM AND READING

O GOD, we are shaken by terror,
our hearts grow cold through fear.
The lions roar, their teeth are bared,
they pounce at our throats and tear us apart.

The powers that be stand over us,
whispering treason to workers for peace,
declaring redundant the awkward and angular,
destroying by rumour the worth of a name.

Old loyalties no longer bind us,
family, neighbourhood, union, factory.
The young prowl the streets and the precincts,
alienated, rootless, pain turning to violence.
And the old, the weak, and the poor all cringe,
their welfare, their lives, threatened and vulnerable.

Your will for us, dear God, is sure and steady,
that we do justly, love mercy, and walk humbly
    in your Way.
You would not have us return evil for evil,
plundering our enemies and requiting our friends.

Who can stand in your presence
with righteousness and integrity of heart?
Our hearts and our minds conceive evil:
they are pregnant with mischief and bring forth lies.

We cannot but sense your love as your wrath,
Judge of the earth come with dread to save us.
Who can stand against the blast of your fury,
fiery shafts sprung from your bow?
Who can bear the anguish and pain in your eyes,
as you scour and cleanse us with lasers?

And yet we give you thanks and praise,
for you will not let us go into the void.
You bear the cost of our redeeming,
the Judge of all the world does right,
bringing us through tears to love for our neighbour,
leading us in pathways to glory and peace.

JESUS saw a poor widow put two copper coins into the treasury, and
he said: "Truly I tell you, this poor widow has put in more than all
the others; for they contributed out of their abundance, but she out
of her poverty has put in all the living that she had."

DAY 3: PSALM AND READING

WHAT are they now but a name,
the empires of old that have vanished?
What are they now but ruins,
cities that gleamed with pride?
Where will our idolatry end?
How many more succumb to the engines of war?

You that wept for Jerusalem,
that knew not what made for its peace,
see now your prophecy extend
as we enter the eclipse of our God.

We stare dumbly at the death camps of hell:
lo! dark Evil is crowned
in the midst of the tortured and dying.
The needy are forgotten,
the oppressed know not the stronghold of God.

The hope of the weary grows dim:
the heavens are empty;
no ear hears the moan of those stricken down
beneath a pitiless sky.

O God, do you not hear the hard-pressed cries?
Have you forgotten? When will you listen?
How long must we endure, how long?

But I will not give in to despair,
for you came to your people of old,
in desert and exile, betrayal and death,
giving joy and great hope,
the light of your Presence
in the least expected of places.

Even from the depths of our doom
comes the cry of the victory of God.

GOD so loved the world that he gave his only Son, that whoever
believes in him should not perish but have eternal life. For God sent
the Son into the world, not to condemn the world, but that the
world might be saved through him.

DAY 4: PSALM AND READING

In arrogance we rich have pursued the poor:
let us be trapped in the schemes we devised.
We have boasted of the desires of our hearts:
greedy for gain we have renounced you, O God.

Our mouths were full of cursing and scoffing;
under our tongues were oppression and mischief.
In country lanes we have hidden and pounced,
in city streets we have stalked and murdered.
Our eyes have watched stealthily for the helpless,
we lurked like lions to seize the poor.

We crushed the afflicted, they sank down and fell
under the weight of our frozen hearts.
We denied them a name, we defrauded them of land.
We reduced them to a number, no voice in their destiny.
We thought in our hearts, God has forgotten,
God has turned away and will never see.

At last their cry reaches our ears,
we hear the whisper of a conscience revived.
Call us, O God, to account.
Do not forget the ones we afflicted,
do justice through us to the orphans.

May we strike terror no more.
Break the strength of our arms.
Return us to the ways of justice and law.
Hear the desire of the poor, strengthen their hearts.

We renounce our pride and our greed,
the wickedness that brims with excess.
Defenceless and naked before you,
may we be judged by those we oppressed.
Refine us with fire, purge us with truth,
bring us at last to your mercy.

JESUS said: "It is easier for a camel to go through the eye of a needle than for a rich man to enter the kingdom of God. . .Truly I say to you, there is no man who has left home or spouse or brothers or sisters or parents or children, for the sake of the kingdom of God, who will not receive manifold more in this time, and in the age to come eternal life."

DAY 5: PSALM AND READING

As a hazelnut lies in the palm of my hand,
so I rest secure in the Presence of God.
Yet I fear the fanatics who toy with the trigger,
oiling their rifles with consummate care,
ready to pounce in the dimly lit alley,
raping the makers of peace and of justice.

But to flee like a bird to the mountains –
no safety in the caves of the earth in our day;
the very foundations are splitting apart,
there is nowhere to go but the place where we are.

I turn again in your presence, dear God,
seeking to renew my trust in your care.
For we tremble and shake, gripped by that fear:
the world we have known is crumbling around us,
invisible rain falls on the mountains,
even the caves of the earth fill with rubble.

Within the future that is coming to meet us,
your presence is steadily with us, O God.
Though you seem so remote in our days,
turning your back, dead to the world,
yet we believe that you hold us in mind,
purging us of violence and hardness of heart,
raining coals of fire on our wickedness,
burning up our fury in your own scorching wind.

Give us new integrity of heart,
renew in us the deeds that you love,
justice and mercy, compassion and courage.
Then face to face shall we see you,
knowing and known, loving and loved.

JESUS said: "Your ancestors ate the manna in the wilderness, and they died. This is the bread which comes down from heaven, that men and women may eat of it and not die. I am the living bread which came down from heaven; if you eat of this bread you will live for ever; and the bread which I shall give for the life of the world is my flesh."

DAY 6: PSALM AND READING

WHO speaks any longer the truth of the heart,
words that are clear of corruption and lies?
Neighbour speaks false unto neighbour,
flattery on our lips, deceit in our hearts.
The proud, silver-tongued with smooth words,
control the dumb and the awkward of speech.

O God, cut out the forked tongue,
silence the lying lips.
Save us from the corruption of language,
from manipulators of words, greedy for power.
For we drown in menacing lies;
the spring of original falsehood
now swells to torrent and spate.

May the exiles and migrants, denied their own language,
find living words to shape their own truth,
words that give meaning to lives without purpose,
that heal and inspire and reach deep in the heart.
Speak to us out of your silence, O God,
our minds purged of gossip and chatter.
For you are the fountain of all that is true,
a wellspring deep that never fails.

It is there that we drink long of your Word,
as sure as a friend who is tested and tried.
For your promise is true and worthy of trust,
like silver refined in the furnace.

JESUS stood up and proclaimed: "Let those who are thirsty come
to me and drink. If you believe in me, as the scripture has said,
'Out of your heart shall flow rivers of living water'."

DAY 7: PSALM AND READING

How long, O God, how long?
You hide your face from me,
you utterly forget me.

How long, O God, how long?
My being is in anguish and torment,
my heart is grieved day and night.

How long, O God, how long?
Icy death, dread and despair,
insidious foes, they strengthen their grip.

Dull are my eyes and lifeless,
as I stare at the desolate places.
Give light to my eyes,
stir up my will and my passion,
my trust in your life-giving Spirit.

Fill my heart with compassion and strength,
that I may rejoice in your generous love,
able to strive with my foes,
no longer dead in the depths of my being.

Yes, at the moment of emptiness and dread
you surprise me with joy and deliverance.
I will sing and shout with delight,
for you have overwhelmed me with grace.

JESUS said: "You call me Teacher and Lord; and you are right, for so I am. If I then your Lord and Teacher have washed your feet, you ought to wash one another's feet. For I have given you an example, that you also should do as I have done to you. I tell you truly, servants are not greater than their masters; nor are those who are sent greater than the one who sent them. If you know these things, blessed are you if you do them".

DAY 8: PSALM AND READING

My enemies encircle me to put me in chains:
they have closed their hearts to pity,
their mouths speak pride and arrogance.
They track me down and surround me on every side,
watching how to bring me to the ground.
They are like lions greedy for their prey,
like young lions lurking in ambush.

Though I trust I am safe in your presence, O God,
yet am I afraid, there is terror in my heart.
Arise, O God, stand in their way, cast them down:
deliver me from the wicked by the power of your sword.
Slay them with your iron fist,
may they choke on the grapes of your wrath . . .

O God, like the psalmist of old I am angry
at the ways of the brutal on earth:
afraid of their malice and greed,
I tremble on the point of their sword.

Yet the hammer of my words and cries
is held in my hands, poised in the air.
For I know the evil in my heart,
the lying, the pride, and the arrogance.

Purge me of hatred and smugness,
of self-righteous satisfied smile.
Help me to love my enemies with truth,
for we are all children of your love.

> Even as I pray for your Justice,
> for the vindication of your Promise,
> that oppressors may triumph no more,
> that their victims may run free in the wind,
> so I pray for their deliverance too.
> Save us through judgment and mercy,
> dependent as we are on your faithfulness.

JESUS said: "If you continue in my word, you are truly my disciples, and you will know the truth, and the truth will make you free."

DAY 9: PSALM AND READING

GOD of Abraham and Sarah, God of our ancestors,
creating among us your realm and your glory,
> bless those who rule on the people's behalf,
> give them strength in the time of our troubles.

Send them the help of your light and your wisdom,
give them support through the prayers of our hearts.
> Remember their promise to serve all the people,
> take from them their lust for power and for wealth.

Remember our promise to serve others' good,
accept the sacrifice of lives that are broken.
> Give to your people the desire of their hearts,
> fulfilling within them all that they cherish.

We shout for joy for your blessings towards us,
we lift high the Cross in the name of our God.
> For you saved us with the power of unbroken love,
> and indeed you fulfil what we deeply desire.

May the rulers of the people acknowledge your name,
serve the common good in the light of your justice.
> Some put their trust in weapons of war,
> but we shall trust in the power of your name.
> They will rust, collapse, and decay,
> but those strong in God will endure through the days.

May those who lead us trust you, O God,
give them wisdom to lead through laws that are just.
For you will answer our prayer in the day of our cry,
fulfilling your nature and your own lasting name.

JESUS said: "If you love me, you will keep my commandments. And
I will pray the Father, and he will give you another Counsellor, to
be with you for ever, even the Spirit of truth, whom the world
cannot receive, because it neither sees him nor knows him; you
know him, for he dwells with you, and will be in you."

DAY 10: PSALM AND READING

FROM the depths of despair I cried out,
seared with pain and with grief.
Where are you, O God?
How long must I suffer?

You drew me up from the deeps,
like a prisoner out of a dungeon,
a flesh-body touched by your hand,
flickering and trembling with life.

You brought me out of a land full of gloom,
a place of hollow silence and cold.
You melted my paralyzed fear:
the warmth of your Sun coursed through my veins.

The wrath of your love lasts but a moment,
for a lifetime your mercy and healing.
Heaviness and weeping last through the night,
yet day breaks into singing and joy.

I will praise you, O God,
for you have made me whole.
I will give you thanks
in the midst of your people.

JESUS said: "Truly I say to you, I am the door of the sheep. . . If you enter by me, you will be saved, and you will go in and out and find pasture. . . I came that they may have life, and have it abundantly. . . I am the good shepherd; I know my own and my own know me, as the Father knows me and I know the Father; and I lay down my life for the sheep. And I have other sheep, that are not of this fold; I must bring them also, and they will heed my voice. So there shall be one flock, one shepherd."

DAY 11: PSALM AND READING

IN the strength you gave me I felt secure,
built upon rock, firm as the hills.
Basking in the warmth of your favour,
the prosperity of my days increased.

I slipped into the worship of money,
the goods of this world ensnaring me.
They gathered like a turbulent cloud,
blotting out the sight of your face.

Then I was greatly dismayed,
feeling foolish in toppling pride,
unable to praise you from the wasteland of hell,
to proclaim your name from the graveyards of death.

O God, have mercy upon me,
forgive my self-satisfied pride,
disentangle the web I have woven,
patiently probe me with the scalpel of truth.

You turn my lamentation to dancing,
lifting me to my feet, clothing me with joy.
In the depths of my being I explode into laughter,
and sing with gratitude the triumph of love.

JESUS said: "Truly I say to you, you will weep and lament, but the world will rejoice; you will be sorrowful, but your sorrow will turn into joy. When a woman is in travail she has sorrow, because her hour has come; but when she is delivered of the child, she no longer remembers the anguish, for joy that a child is born into the world."

DAY 12: PSALM AND READING

O GOD, do you rebuke me in your anger?
Do you chasten me in fierce displeasure?
Is it your arrows that pierce me,
your hand come heavy upon me?
With no health in my flesh, do you punish me,
in sternness of love, for my sins?

The tide of my wrongs sweeps over my head,
their weight is a burden too heavy to bear.
My wounds stink and fester through folly,
I am bowed down with grieving all the day long.
My loins are filled with a burning pain,
there is no sound part in my flesh.
I am numbed and stricken to the ground,
I groan in the anguish of my heart.

The pounding of my heart comes to your ears,
my desire for love, my stumblings on the road.
My deep sighing is not hidden from you,
my longing for kindness and the touch that heals.
My heart is in tumult, my strength fails me,
even the light of my eyes has gone from me.

I am like the deaf and hear nothing,
like those whose mouths are sealed.
I have become as one who cannot hear,
in whose mouth there is no retort.

But in you, O God, I have put my trust,
and you will answer me in saving judgment.
Do not forsake me, do not go far from me:
hasten to my help, O God of my salvation.

For I know you enter the heart of our anguish,
you take to yourself the pain of the universe,
you bear the effects of our sins,
you endure and still you forgive.

It is not for our sin that we suffer,
nor for the wrongs of our ancestors.
It is that your name may be glorified,
that in us your purpose may be known.
Your vulnerable love works without ceasing,
to draw us from despair into glory.

JESUS said: "It was not that this man sinned, or his parents, that he was born blind, but that the works of God might be made manifest in him. We must work the works of the One who sent me, while it is day; night comes, when no one can work. As long as I am in the world, I am the light of the world."

DAY 13: PSALM AND READING

BLESSED are those who care for the poor and the helpless,
who are kind to the outcast within them.
God will deliver them in the day of their trouble,
rescuing the child who is battered and torn.

O God, you will not give us over to the will of our enemies,
to hatred within and to blame without.
In the day of our calamity you will sustain us,
as warring turbulence threatens our life.

Dear God, be merciful towards me,
heal me for I have sinned against you.
My enemies, within and without, speak evil of me:
"When will you die and your name perish for ever?"

They smile at the revealing of my sins,
gloating in triumph at my downfall,
cackling like demons that claw at me,
plucking me down to the mire.

"You are wracked with a deadly disease,
you will not rise again from where you lie."
Even my bosom friend whom I trusted,
who shared my bread, looks down on me.

O God, come down and raise me up,
struggling from the pit in anger and truth,
wrestling with my enemies in love for them,
dependent together on mercy.
So shall we know that you delight in us,
setting us before your face for ever.

Cleanse my whole being that I may see truly,
that revenge may not brood in my heart.
Keep me from believing all strangers are hostile,
let me see with eyes of compassion.

May I think good of those who strive against me,
however full of malice seem their hearts.
Heap burning coals of love on our heads:
melt our fears with the flame of your desire.

Burn out from us all that breeds evil,
that we may no longer hurt or destroy.
May we follow the way of your justice,
and be redeemed to your glory and joy.

JESUS said: "A new commandment I give to you, that you love one
another; even as I have loved you, that you also love one another.
By this all folk will know that you are my disciples, if you have love
for one another."

DAY 14: PSALM AND READING

O GOD, you are greatly to be praised
in the city of your dwelling place.
High and beautiful is the holy mountain,
it is the joy of the whole earth.

Here on Mount Zion stands the city
where you reign with just and steady hand.
Your rule is firm and secure,
strong as the walls and ramparts.

We call your mercies to mind,
here in the midst of your temple.
You govern the peoples with justice,
even to the ends of the earth.

So may we tell those who come after,
that here they may rest secure,
for our God reigns for ever and ever,
who will guide us to all eternity. . .

Such was the place of your worship and dwelling,
sacred, O God, to your people of old.
Now may you dwell in each of our hearts,
may every city be the place of your dwelling.

So may we worship you in spirit and truth,
may recognize you in streets and in squares,
in a common life of justice and peace,
in compassion and freedom under the law.

Bring the light, O God, that will one day shine
brighter than the sun and the moon and the stars,
the light of the Christ to illumine the dark,
the face that transfigures the city to glory.

JESUS said: "Truly I say to you, those who believe in me will also
do the works that I do; and greater works than these they will do,
because I go to the Father. Whatever you ask in my name, I will do
it, that the Father may be glorified in the Son; if you ask anything
in my name, I will do it."

DAY 15: PSALM AND READING

So often the powerful ones of the world
seem to boast of their mischief and pride.
They trust in the abundance of wealth,
they take perverse delight in their greed.

They contrive destroying slanders;
their tongue cuts sharp like a razor.
They love words that hurt and devour,
and every deceit of the tongue.

They step on one another as they climb to power,
they thrust the weak to the gutter;
seducing the gullible in smooth magic of words,
they trample the truth in their pursuit of ambition.

O God, break them down utterly,
uproot them from the land of the living,
topple them from their Babel of lies,
throw them down to the dust!

Yet so often we are the powerful,
if only with family and friends.
We wound with whispers of gossip,
mockery and scorn in our hearts,
bitterness souring our lips.

Too easy to call on God to destroy,
hard to be humbled by words that are true.
And even as we cry for the righting of wrongs,
for the destruction of those who harm others,
so do we know that revenge solves nothing,
annihilation reaping more violence still.

May your Spirit go deeper within us,
purging our hearts, burning the impure.
Hold at bay our murderous words.
May we strive with the angel of justice,
living the way of your truth and your word,
our faces etched in the fierceness of love.

JESUS said of the woman who had washed his feet with her tears and
her hair and her ointment: "Her sins which are many are forgiven
for she loved much; but the one who is forgiven little, loves little."
And he said to her, "Your sins are forgiven. . .Your faith has saved
you; go in peace."

DAY 16: PSALM AND READING

It was not an enemy who taunted me,
or I might have been able to bear it.
It was not a foe who was so insolent,
or I might have hidden myself away.

But it was you, my equal,
my companion, my familiar friend.
Ours was a pleasant harmony,
as we walked side by side to the house of our God.

You have not kept your word,
you have no love of God in your heart,
you have broken the covenant you have sworn,
deserting those who were at peace with you.

Your mouth is smooth as butter,
yet war is in your heart.
Your words are softer than oil,
yet your sword flashes in the dark.

My heart cries out in anguish and grief,
Get out of my sight, you hypocrite!
Go down in terror to your grave, you betrayer!
For you have worked treachery among us.

Yet how I yearn for the healing of pain,
for a love grown cold to kindle again.
I pray to you, God, that we may be reconciled,
drawn again to the way of your justice.

Humble the pride in us all,
your love and your power consistent for ever.
May we lift the weight of oppression,
may our enemies release the spring of their traps.

I cast my burden on you, O God,
and you will sustain and encourage me.
I will call from the midst of my groaning,
you will redeem me to healing and peace.

My heart has been so constricted,
my affections so easily hurt.
Yet your arms are wide and welcoming,
in your presence we are released,
and feel strangely at home.

JESUS said: "In the world you will have tribulation; but be of good
courage, I have overcome the world."

DAY 17: PSALM AND READING

I PRAY for the tortured and victims of malice,
for those imprisoned for no fault of their own.
My feelings run high – God forgive the excess –
why is your mercy and justice delayed?

Deliver the oppressed from the terrors of evil,
free them from those who relish their pain.
For the savage stir up violence against them,
waiting to knock at the door before dawn.

They keep the peacemakers distracted and tense,
breaking their spirit and mauling their flesh,
and all for no sin or transgression,
or any crime for which they are guilty.

The oppressed look to you, O God, their strength:
arise from your sleep and do not delay.
May your eyes flash with judgment and truth,
silencing the treacherous and false.

In your great love run to meet those who suffer,
show them the downfall of those who trod on them.
Yet slay not the wicked, copying their ways,
but make them powerless, and bring them to truth.

O God, from the depths of your love bearing pain,
break the cycle of our wraths and our sorrows.
For you are not a God who destroys;
you seek always to redeem and renew.

And so I will sing of your love and your power,
I will sing in the morning and tell of your goodness.
For you have been our strong tower,
a sure refuge in the day of distress.
I will sing your praise, O God my strength,
for you are my kraal for ever.

JESUS said: "I am the light of the world; if you follow me you will
not walk in darkness, but will have the light of life."

DAY 18: PSALM AND READING

IN the depths of my being I become quiet and still:
I wait for you, my God, source of my salvation.
You are a sure and steady rock watching over me,
so that I shall not fall to my doom.

I am afraid of the powerful who overwhelm me,
cowards who encircle me, towering above me.
They are like a battering ram to a crumbling wall,
they exult in their lust for destruction.

Their delight is only in lies:
the truth is far from their hearts.
They utter words that are softer than butter:
inwardly they do but curse.

Nevertheless I hold steadily to you:
you are my hope, my rock, my salvation.
In the stillness I wait for your presence:
you watch over me: I shall not fall to my doom.

In you, O God, is my health and glory,
the rock of my faith; in you is my trust.
I pour out my whole being in your presence,
and in you do I put all my hope.

In very truth we are but a breath of wind;
faithless and fearful, we have betrayed you.
Put us in the balance and we can only rise:
we are lighter than a feather in the breeze.

Let us not trust in extortion and robbery,
let us not put on the masks of vanity.
When riches and possessions increase,
let us not set our heart upon them.

For then we should become like the powerful,
betraying you again with our love of money,
trampling the face of the poor in the mire,
holding on to wealth by means of the lie.

Teach me again, O God, the truth of your name:
to you alone belongs power,
in you alone do we find mercy.
What reward could there be for our work?

JESUS said: "Those who believe in me, believe not in me, but in the One who sent me. And those who see me see the One who sent me. I have come as light into the world, that those who believe in me may not remain in darkness. If you hear my sayings and do not keep them, I do not judge you; for I did not come to judge the world but to save the world. Those who reject me and do not receive my sayings have a judge: the word that I have spoken will be their judge on the last day."

DAY 19: PSALM AND READING

In the depths of my being you are my God.
At the rising of the sun I seek your face.
My heart thirsts for you, my flesh longs for you,
in a barren and dry land where no water is.

I search for you in unexpected places,
at the edge of the known, in the language of dreams,
in the wilderness of the city streets,
in the grim towers where the desperate dwell.

There may I look long and lovingly,
there may I listen for a Word behind words.
There may I wait for a glimpse of your glory,
there may I utter strange songs of your praise.

For your love endures to the end,
it is better even than life itself.
So shall my lips praise you,
and I shall lift up my hands in your name.

With manna in my exile do you feed me,
with water springing up from parched land.
I am deeply satisfied as with a sumptuous feast,
my whole being resonates with sounds of joy.

Courage have I found to face the creatures of the night,
the terrible faces that mask a helpless cry,
swords that glint in the darkness,
jackals that swoop on their prey.

I am bewildered by mirrors of distortion,
helpless before hallucinations in the sun.
Yet will I trust you through the blindness of the light,
through the delusions that threaten to destroy me.

I hear your voice, Do not be afraid.
You sustain me in the watches of the night,
your hovering wings protect me on my journey,
I stumble yet I trust you to hold me.

So shall I come to the place of rejoicing,
and see your face in all your creatures.
The mouths of the liars will be silenced:
even they will speak the truth from their hearts.

JESUS said: "I have yet many things to say to you, but you cannot bear them now. When the Spirit of truth comes, he will guide you into all the truth; for he will not speak on his own authority, but whatever he hears he will speak and he will declare to you the things that are to come. He will glorify me, for he will take what is mine and declare it to you."

DAY 20: PSALM AND READING

How lovely are your dwellings, O God,
how beautiful are the holy places.
In the days of my pilgrimage I yearn for them:
they are the temples of your living presence.
I have a desire and longing to enter my true home:
my heart and my flesh rejoice in the living God.

For the sparrow has found a house for herself,
and the swallow a nest where she may lay her young.
Even so are those who dwell in your house –
they will always be praising you.
And yet your Spirit dwells within us:
may we recognize you and welcome your Presence.

Blessed are those whose strength is in you,
in whose heart are your ways,
who trudging through the plains of misery find in them
    a well,
and the pools are filled with water.

They become springs of healing for others,
reservoirs of compassion to those who are bruised.
Strengthened themselves they lend courage to others,
and God will be there at the end of their journey.

O God of our ancestors, hear my prayer,
guide me as you did your servants of old.
Bless those who govern on the people's behalf,
keep us close to your will and your ways.

One day lived in your presence
is better than a thousand in my own dwelling.
I had rather beg in the burning sun
on the threshold of the house of my God
than sit in cool courtyards
of luxury and worldly success.

For you are my light and my shield,
you will give me your grace and your glory.
You are ready with bountiful gifts,
overflowing to those who follow you.

Living God of love,
blessed are those who put their trust in you.

JESUS said: "Abide in me, and I in you. As the branch cannot bear fruit by itself, unless it abides in the vine, neither can you unless you abide in me. I am the vine, you are the branches. Those who abide in me, and I in them, those are they who bear much fruit, for apart from me you can do nothing."

DAY 21: PSALM AND READING

O GOD, sovereign of the universe,
you have put on robes of glory:
you have shone with the apparel of light,
and girded yourself with the strength of earth.
You have made the round world so sure,
within the bounds of your compassionate power.

Ever since the world began
your reign has been prepared:
for you are the eternal Creator.

The seas have risen, O God,
the oceans have lift up their voice,
the seas hurl their pounding waves.
The breakers of the sea are mighty,
the waves rage horribly.

But you, great God of the universe,
you reign for ever and ever.
Your promises, O God, are very sure:
holiness adorns you house for ever.

And where do we now see your power?
In a man afflicted and stricken,
cast out of the city, betrayed by his friends,
holiness in a love that endures,
glory through the wounds and the pain.

How awesome are your deeds, O God,
how wonderful are the works that create and redeem.

JESUS said: "This is eternal life, that they know thee the only true God, and Jesus Christ whom thou hast sent. I glorified thee on earth, having accomplished the work which thou gavest me to do; and now, Father, glorify thou me in thy own presence with the glory which I had with thee before the world was made."

DAY 22: PSALM AND READING

SING to the great God a new song,
sing to the Creator, sing the whole earth.

We sing to you, God, and praise your name,
telling of your salvation from day to day,
declaring your glory to those who do not know you,
and your wonders to the peoples of the earth.

Marvellous God, you are greatly to be praised,
more to be honoured than all the powers.
Glory and worship are before you,
power and honour are in your sanctuary.

May we, the household of your people,
ascribe to you worship and glory,
giving you the honour due to your name,
bringing presents as we come into your house.

We worship you in the beauty of holiness:
let the whole earth stand in awe of you.

Let us tell it out among the peoples that you are God,
and that you are making the round world so sure,
held within the bounds of your love,
and that you will judge the peoples righteously.

Let the heavens rejoice and let the earth be glad:
let the sea roar, and all its creatures delight:
let the fields be joyful, and all that is in them:
then shall the trees of the wood shout for joy.

For you come to judge the earth,
with justice to make right what is wrong,
to judge the peoples with your truth.

JESUS found Philip and said to him, "Follow me.". . . Philip found
Nathanael, and said to him, "We have found him of whom
Moses. . . and the prophets wrote, Jesus of Nazareth, the son of
Joseph." Nathanael said to him, "Can anything good come out of
Nazareth?" Philip said to him, "Come and see." Jesus saw
Nathanael coming to him, and said of him, "Behold, an Israelite
indeed, in whom is no guile!"

DAY 23: PSALM AND READING

WE praise you, O God, with a new song,
for you have done marvellous things.

With your own right hand,
and with your holy arm,
with the strength of weakness
and the enduring of waiting,
you have achieved the greatest of victories,
bringing triumph from the midst of defeat.

So you have declared your salvation,
showing justice in the sight of the peoples.

You have remembered your mercy and faithfulness
towards the house of Israel,
and all the ends of the world have seen your salvation.

Show yourselves joyful in God, all you peoples,
sing, rejoice, and give thanks.

We praise you, O God, upon the harp,
singing a psalm of thanksgiving,
with trumpets and echoing horns,
showing ourselves joyful in your presence.

Let the sea roar, and all its creatures,
the round earth and those who dwell on it.
Let the streams clap their hands,
and let the hills be joyful before you.

For you have come to judge the earth,
justified at last in your sight,
and judging the peoples with justice,
with a mercy beyond our comparing,
O holy, compassionate, and most loving God.

JESUS said: "My kingship is not of this world... For this I was born,
and for this I have come into the world, to bear witness to the truth.
Every one who is of the truth hears my voice."

DAY 24: PSALM AND READING

WE praise you, O God,
and give you thanks for you are good,
and your mercies endure for ever.

Great deeds have you done to rescue us,
and we praise your name for ever and ever.

Yet we have sinned like our ancestors,
we did not destroy the heathen
as you commanded us to do...

Did you command your people to destroy,
to commit even genocide according to your will?

Were they so utterly evil
that not one of them deserved to survive?

Despite the rebellion of our ancestors,
you spared them and graced them still.

Is your covenant only for a few who are favoured,
flourishing at the expense of the many?

In our day such thoughts are too proud,
too dangerous for our fragile earth home.

Your covenant is with all that you have made,
loving all creation through pain to its glory.

Yes, we might suffer through our folly and greed,
through the devilish blindness and malice of old:

yet your power, not almighty in magic,
neither capricious nor blind in its force,
will sustain and redeem your world yet,

witholding your fierce scalding fire,
refining in the heat of your love,
bringing out of evil unimaginable good.

JESUS said to the disciples: "Peace be with you. As the Father has
sent me, even so I send you." And when he had said this, he
breathed on them, and said to them, "Receive the Holy Spirit. If
you forgive the sins of any, they are forgiven; if you retain the sins
of any, they are retained."

DAY 25: PSALM AND READING

THEY that go down to the sea in ships,
or take to the air in great birds,
these folk see your works,
your wonders in the deep and in the skies.

For at your word the stormy wind arises,
lifting the waves of the sea,
stirring the turbulent clouds.
They are carried up to the heavens,
and down again to the depths.
They are tossed to and fro in peril.
They reel and stagger like drunkards,
and their craftsmanship is in vain.

Then they cry to you, God, in their trouble,
and you deliver them from their distress.

Storms within and without cease at your word,
the waves of the sea and the air are stilled.
They recover their poise, panic leaves them,
they discover a presence that guides them through.

Then they are glad, because they are at rest,
and you bring them to the haven where they would be.

O that folk would therefore praise you for your goodness,
and declare the wonders that you do for the children of
   earth.
At the gathering of the congregation your name be
   praised!
From the seat of the elders may you be glorified!

JESUS said: "I am the way, the truth, and the life. No one comes to
the Father but by me. If you had known me, you would have known
my Father also; henceforth you know him and have seen him."

DAY 26: PSALM AND READING

My heart is fixed on you, O God,
my soul's desire directed towards you.

Awake, my soul, awake flute and harp:
I will make melody to awaken the morning.

I will give you thanks, O God, among the peoples:
I will sing your praise among the nations.
For the greatness of your mercy reaches to the skies,
and your faithfulness to the clouds.

Be exalted, O God, above the heavens,
and let your glory be over all the earth,
that those whom you love may be delivered.
O save us by your right hand and answer me.

Who will lead me into the fortified city?
Who will bring me to the place you have promised?
Have you cast us off, O God?
You do not go out with our armies.

Give us your help against the enemy,
for vain is any human help.
By the power of our God we shall do valiantly,
for it is you that will tread down our enemies...

So are we blind to your deepest desire,
assuming that we are your favourites.
O God, triumph now in the way of your Christ,
bring to fruit the seeds of his non-violent passion,
absorbing evil in love's fiery crucible,
disarming the powers and loving his enemies.
So may your reign be known through the world,
the very need for enemies banished for ever.

JESUS said: "Martha, Martha, you are anxious and troubled about many things: one thing is needful. Mary has chosen the good portion, which shall not be taken away from her."

DAY 27: PSALM AND READING

I PRAISE you, O God,
I praise you with my whole heart,
in the company of the redeemed
and among the congregation.

Your works are marvellous and vast,
contemplated by all who delight in them,
desert and mountain, ocean and moor,
stretching beyond the range of our eyes.

Your deeds are majestic and glorious,
your justice stands for ever.

Your marvellous acts of deliverance and rescue
have won you a name to be treasured for ever.

Indeed you are gracious and merciful.
You give food to those who love you,
you remember your covenant for ever.

You showed the people the power of your deeds,
you gave them a share in the stewardship of earth.

The works of your hands are faithful and just,
and all your commandments are sure.

They stand firm for ever and ever,
they are done in faithfulness and truth.

You sent redemption to your people,
you ordained your covenant for ever:
holy is your name and worthy to be feared.

The fear of the Lord is the beginning of wisdom,
of good understanding are those who keep your
  commandments.
Your praise shall endure for ever.

JESUS said: "Are not five sparrows sold for two pennies? And not one of them is forgotten before God. Why, even the hairs of your head are all numbered. Fear not: you are of more value than many sparrows."

DAY 28: PSALM AND READING

IT is not to our name that praise is due,
but to yours, eternal God of love,
for you are faithful and kind and merciful.

Why do we say, Where now is our God?
For you are far beyond us,
surpassing us in wisdom and care.

Our idols are silver and gold,
even the works of our hands.

They have mouths but they speak not:
eyes have they, but they see not.
They have ears, but they do not hear,
they have noses, but they do not smell.
With their hands they do not feel,
and with their feet they do not walk.
Neither is there any sound in their throat.
Their makers grow to be like them,
and so do all who put their trust in them.

But we put our trust in you, O God:
you give us courage to face our enemies.

You remember us and you bless us:
you bless all who hold you in honour,
both small and great.

You are with us and for us
and for our children after us.

Creator of the universe, you bless each one of us.
Far beyond the stars, you give us the earth to care for.
So will we praise you from this time forth,
even for evermore. Alleluia.

JESUS said: "The Kingdom of God is like a grain of mustard seed which a man took and sowed in his garden; and it grew and became a tree, and the birds of the air made nests in its branches. . .The Kingdom of God is like leaven which a woman took and hid in three measures of meal, till it was all leavened."

DAY 29: PSALM AND READING

I WAS glad when they said to me,
Let us go to the house of God.

And now our feet are standing
within your gates, O Jerusalem:
Jerusalem which is built as a city,
where the pilgrims gather in unity.

There the people go up,
drawn on by love of your name:

there is the seat of judgment and mercy,
the place of your grace, O God.

O pray for the peace of Jerusalem,
may those who love you prosper.

Peace be within your walls,
and prosperity in your households.

For the sake of friends and companions
I will pray that peace may be with you.

For the sake of the house of our God
I will seek for your good.

JESUS said to the twelve, "Will you also go away?" Simon Peter
answered him, "Lord, to whom shall we go? You have the words
of eternal life; and we have believed, and come to know, that you
are the Holy One of God."

DAY 30: PSALMS AND READING

DEAR God, my heart is not proud,
nor are my eyes haughty.
I do not busy myself in great matters,
nor in what is beyond me.
But I have calmed and quieted my very being:
my soul is like a child
smiling and tranquil at the mother's breast.

O descendants of Israel, let us praise God
from this time forth and for ever.

BROTHERS and sisters, friends of God,
how joyful and good a thing it is –
like the gathering of a mountain range –
to dwell together in unity.

It is like a precious and fragrant oil,
like the dew of early morning,
or the scent of summer in the forest,
like the peace of the holy places
where God gives us great blessing
and promises life for evermore.

JESUS said: "I do not pray only for those whom thou didst give to
me, but also for those who believe in me through their word, that
they may all be one, even as thou, Father, art in me, and I in thee,
that they also may be in us, so that the world may believe that thou
hast sent me."

DAY 31: PSALM AND READING

BY the waters of Babylon we sat down and wept
when we remembered you, O Zion.
As for our harps we hid them away
in the thickets of the willow.

For they that led us away captive
required of us a song,
a melody in our heaviness.
"Sing us one of the songs of Zion."
How shall we sing the Lord's song in a strange land?

If I forget you, O Jerusalem,
let my right hand wither away.

If I do not remember you,
let my tongue cleave to the roof of my mouth –
yes, if I do not prefer Jerusalem to my dearest joy.

Great anger rises within me, a thirst for revenge
against those who have destroyed our city.

"May your children be hurled against the rocks,
even as we watch . . ."

O God, forgive my rage,
however righteous is my indignation.
Turn my heart to forgiveness,
our captors to repentance.

Work in us deeds of your grace,
justice for all the oppressed,
a new heart for all the oppressors.
May we not return evil for evil,
but strive with them till all of us are blessed.

JESUS said: "The kingdom of heaven is like treasure hidden in a
field, which a man found and covered up; then in his joy he goes
and sells all that he has and buys that field. Again, the kingdom of
heaven is like a merchant in search of fine pearls, who, on finding
one pearl of great price, went and sold all that he had and bought
it."

CANTICLE FOR SUNDAY: EASTER ANTHEMS

WE praise you, O Christ,
risen from the dead,
breaking death's dominion,
rising from the grave.
Absorbing in yourself
the force of evil's ways,
you destroyed death's age-old sting,
and now you are alive for evermore.

Let us find our life in you,
breaking through our fear
of everlasting void.
For you are risen from the dead,
first fruits of those who sleep.

From the days of first awareness
we betrayed the call of life,
yet yearned for that communion
which still we dimly sense.

Pain and evil, malice and cruel greed,
these deepened the sorrow of our hearts.
Yet they are done away
in light of glorious dawn,
the victory of resurrection day.

At one with all who've lived,
so all of us have died;
at one with your humanity,
all shall be made alive.

CANTICLE FOR MONDAY: TE DEUM

MEN and women: praise the God of Love!
Earth and sky: worship the Creator!

Angels, heavenly powers, cherubim and seraphim,
raise the everlasting shout:
Holy, holy, holy, great God of power and love,
the whole creation is full of your glory.

Glorious company of apostles: Alleluia!
Honoured fellowship of prophets: Alleluia!
White-robed gathering of martyrs: Alleluia!

Communion of saints in all times and places
proclaim the glorious Name:
Giver of life, of splendour and wonder!
Bearer of pain, graceful and true!
Maker of love, flaming and passionate!

Christ, we greet you in your glory,
hidden deep in the being of God,
Word made flesh to deliver us,
glad to be born of Mary,

destroying the sting of death,
opening the road to the presence of God,
guarding the freedom of the creation,
yearning for the gathering of the harvest.

Come, then, judge and deliver us,
who are freed at the cost of your life,
and lead us with all your saints
to lands of eternal glory.

CANTICLE FOR TUESDAY: BENEDICTUS

LET us praise Yahweh, the God of Israel!

You came to a people imprisoned, and set them free;
you raised up for us a mighty deliverer,
a descendant of your servant David.

Such was your promise, long, long ago,
by the lips of your holy prophets,
that you would deliver us from our enemies,
from the grip of those who hate us.

This was the covenant with Abraham our father,
that you would treat us with mercy and give us freedom,
that we might serve you without fear,
with integrity and courage our whole life long.

Child, you shall be called the Prophet of the Highest,
you will go before Yahweh to prepare the Way,
leading God's People to knowledge of salvation
through forgiveness of their sins.

For in the tender mercy of our God
the rising sun will shine upon us,
to give light to those who dwell in darkness and in the
    shadow of death,
and to guide our feet into ways of peace.

CANTICLE FOR WEDNESDAY: MAGNIFICAT

My heart is overflowing with praise to my God!
My spirit cries out with joy to my Saviour!
You have looked so tenderly upon me,
your servant from among the poor.
From this day forward all people will call me blessed.
Mighty God, you have done great things for me:
holy indeed is your Name!

Your mercy rests on those who fear you
in every generation.
You have shown the strength of your arm,
scattering the arrogant and proud.
Imperial powers have fallen,
but the poor have been lifted high.
You have filled the hungry with good things,
and left the rich with empty hands.
You have come as you did in times past,
in power to help your servants,
remembering your covenant to Abraham,
faithful to your promise of mercy.

CANTICLE FOR THURSDAY:
THE DIVINE PRAISES

Blessed be God, Holy and most glorious Trinity.
Blessed be God, Creator of the universe.
Blessed be God, Father and Mother.
Blessed be God, Companion and Lover.

Blessed be God, Jesus the Christ,
the same yesterday, today, and for ever.
I Blessed be Christ in us, the hope of glory.
Blessed be God, Holy and life-giving Spirit.
I Blessed be God, Spirit of Wisdom.
Blessed be God, Spirit of Fire
I Blessed be God, moving deep within us.
Blessed be God, spinning the thread of attention
    among us.
I Blessed be God, whose glory is a human being fully alive.
Blessed be God, shining through the saints.
I Blessed be God, shining through the creation.
Blessed be God.

CANTICLE FOR FRIDAY: GREAT AND WONDERFUL

GREAT and wonderful are your deeds, O God of love and
    glory.
Just and true are your ways, O Ruler of the peoples.
Who shall not revere your name? For you alone are holy.
All peoples shall come and worship in your presence,
for your redeeming love has shone in all its glory.
Praise and honour, glory and love,
be given to the One who reigns and to the Lamb.

CANTICLE FOR SATURDAY: SONG OF THE THREE

Refrain   Sing your praise and exalt you for ever.

O GOD of our ancestors, we bless you . . .
We bless your holy and glorious name . . .
We bless you on the heights of the mountains . . .
We bless you in deep and secret places . . .
We bless you in songs of animals and birds . . .
We bless you on the lips of holy people . . .
We bless you in your reign of justice . . .
We bless you, great Trinity of Love . . .

PRAYERS FOR EACH DAY

ETERNAL God, by your power and love you have created and redeemed us: strengthen us in your Spirit that we may give ourselves this day in service and compassion to one another and to you; through Jesus Christ our Saviour.

ETERNAL God, you are the light of the minds that know you, the joy of the hearts that love you, and the strength of the wills that serve you: inspire us so to know you that we may truly love you, and so to love you that we may fully serve you, whom to serve is perfect freedom, in Jesus Christ our Saviour.

CHRIST has no body now on earth but yours, no hands but yours, no feet but yours. Yours are the eyes through which Christ's compassion cares for the people of the world; yours are the feet with which Christ is to go about doing good; yours are the hands through which Christ now brings a blessing.

> GOD bless this city
> and move our hearts with pity
> lest we grow hard.
> God bless this house
> with silence, solitude, and space
> that we may pray.
> God bless these days
> of rough and narrow ways
> lest we despair.
> God bless the night
> and calm the people's fright
> that we may love.
> God bless this land
> and guide us with your hand
> lest we be unjust.
> God bless this earth
> through pangs of death and birth
> and make us whole.

CHRIST be with me, Christ within me,
Christ behind me, Christ before me,
Christ beside me, Christ to win me,
Christ to comfort and restore me.
Christ beneath me, Christ above me,
Christ in quiet, Christ in danger,
Christ in hearts of all that love me,
Christ in mouth of friend and stranger.

> LET nothing disturb you;
> let nothing dismay you.
> All things pass:
> God never changes.
> Patience attains
> all that it strives for.
> Having God
> you will lack nothing.
> God alone suffices.

DEEPEN my roots in the dark earth.
May they spread in silence,
hidden from view.
May I grow steadily like the sturdy oak,
slowly reaching to the sky of my destiny.

MAY I be still and know who you are;
may I walk humbly in your narrow way;
may I run the way of your commandment;
may I leap the dance of those who are set free.

THIS day, dear God,
give me the courage, the will, and the love to say No,
give me the courage, the will, and the love to say Yes,
give me the wisdom to discern when to let my No be No,
   and when to let my Yes be Yes.

> JESUS, watch over me always,
> especially today,
> or I shall betray you.

> GOD, wake me up,
> even though I may not like it.

SOURCES AND ACKNOWLEDGMENTS

PREPARATION

The mental 'directions' for physical posture are derived from the Alexander
Technique.

ADVENT

Opening prayer: Rev.22.20; Is. 40.5; 52.9-10; 7.14; Mt.21.9
Sunday: Is.35; Mk.1.15; NEH16 (Philip Nicolai)
Monday: Is.11.1-8; Rom.13.12; NEH466 (John Marriott)
Tuesday: Is.40.1-9; Jn.1.29-30; NEH12 (Charles Coffin)
Wednesday: Ps.65; Rom.13.11; NEH3 (Charles Wesley)
Thursday: Ps.67; Rev.21.1-7; NEH500 (Frederick Hosmer)
Friday: Ps.80; 1Cor.4.5; NEH9 (Charles Wesley – adapted)
Saturday: Ps.72; Mt.25.35-6; NEH161 (J.B.Peacey)
Cries of Advent: Rev.22 (various); Days 1-6: Trad. (adapted); Days 7-24: Compiler, with
thanks to David Denny & Tessa Bielecki of Nada Hermitage, Crestone, Colorado,
and Mary Robins of Brookmans Park, Hertfordshire, for permission to use
material from their versions.

CHRISTMAS

Introduction: Ps.72.18-9; Lk.1.78-9; Jn.1.14 (adapted); Is.9.6
Psalms, Readings, Hymns: Ps.150 (adapted); Jn.1-14 (paraphrased); Col.1.13-20 (adapted);
NEH24 (John Byrom – adapted); Ps.146; Lk.2.19; Is.9.2.6; NEH41 (Christopher
Smart)
Prayer: The last petition is from the Service of Nine Lessons and Carols at King's
College Chapel, Cambridge.

EPIPHANY

Opening Prayer: Tit.2.11; Is.60.4-5,1; Lk.2.14; Is.52.10
Psalms and Readings: Ps.45; Mt.2.9-12; Ps.47; Lk.10.21-2
Canticle: Rev;21;23; Is.60.1-2; Rev.22.5
Hymn: NEH52 (J.S.B.Monsell)

LENT

Opening prayer: 2Cor.6.4-10
Sunday: Ps.5; Jn.12.24-5; Hos.6.1.-3
Monday: Ps.2; Jn.12.35-6; Hos.6.4-5; Hos.11
Tuesday: Ps.58; Jn.15.1-2; 1Chr.29.10-14
Wednesday: Ps.25; Jn.15.9-11; Is.55.6-11
Thursday: Ps.26; Jn.15.12-5; Mt.5.1-10
Friday: Ps.32; Lk.10.21; Mt.11.28-30
Saturday: Ps.19 (I owe the description of the stars to some words of Ernesto Cardenal, the exact location of which I am unable to trace); Jn.17.15-9; Jn.6.35,50-1,53-8

PASSIONTIDE

First Day: Phil.2.8; Is.53.2-5; Rom.5.8; Ps.31.9-24; 1Cor.1.21-5; Salvator Mundi
Second Day: 1Pet.2.21-5; Is.42.1-8; Rom.5.1-6; Rom.8.37-9
Third Day: Psalm 22 (I owe the thought behind the last two sections on p.67 to Daniel Berrigan's *Uncommon Prayer,* Seabury, 1978, pp.21-22)

EASTER

Opening prayer: Section 2: Eric Milner-White; Section 5: Eph.5.14; Section 6: 1Pet.1.3; Hymn by compiler (can be sung to the tune, *Easter Hymn* or to any other 77.77 metre)
Sunday: Ps.27.7-14; Rom.8.37-9; Easter Anthems; NEH110 (Lyra Davidica)
Monday: Ps.18.1-19; Jn.6.38-9; 1Tim.3.16; NEH107 (Cyril Alington)
Tuesday: Ps.18.25-30, 46-50; Jn.11.25-7; Compiler; NEH102 (P. Dearmer)
Wednesday: Ps.36; Jn.20.17; Col.1.15-20; NEH120 (Edmond Budry)
Thursday: Ps.21; Lk.24.46-8; 1Pet.1.3-8; NEH121 (G.R.Woodward)
Friday: Ps.40; 1Cor.15.51-5; Eph.1.3-10; NEH113 (Charles Wesley)
Saturday: Ps.27.1-6; Jn.14.18-20; Te Deum; NEH112 (Christian Gellert)
Prayer for each day: Prayers of the Taizé Community (adapted)

ASCENSION

Opening Prayer: Heb.2.10; Rom.8.29; Phil.2.5-10
Odd-numbered days: Ps.8; Is.12.2-16; Glory and honour; NEH132 (Christopher Wordsworth – adapted)
Even-numbered days: Ps.24; Is.60.1-3,18-9; Rev.19.1-2,5-7;13.8; NEH401 (Latin 15c.; tr.J.M.Neale)

PENTECOST

Ps.144.28; Jn.3.5-8; 4.13-4; Ezek.36.25-7; 37.9,5-6; NEH137 (Bianco da Siena, tr.R.F.Littledale – adapted)

TRINITY

Ps.90; Eph.1.3,5-6,13-4; NEH146 (R.Heber – adapted); NEH159 (St.Patrick; tr.Mrs.C.F.Alexander)

CREATION
Gen.1.1-2; Jn.1.1-2; Ps.29; Benedicite; Rom.8.18-21; Canticle of the Sun; NEH427 (H.W.Baker)

SAINTS
Rev.1.5; Rom5.2.3; Ps.15; Heb.12.1-2; Rev.2.8,7,10,17,26-8;3.12,21

THE DEPARTED
Russian Kontakion; Ps.16; Rev.21.1-4; Prayers: ASB Proper Preface 16; J.V.Taylor; Last para. of Act of Remembrance: Jewish Act of Remembrance of the Six Million.

ORDINARY DAYS
Opening Psalms: 95; 100

Day 1: Ps.1; Jn.1.36-9
Day 2: Ps.7; Lk.21.2-4
Day 3: Ps.9; Jn.3.16-7
Day 4: Ps.10; Mt.19,.24,29
Day 5: Ps.11; Jn.6.49-51
Day 6: Ps.12; Jn.7.37-8
Day 7: Ps.13; Jn.13.13-7
Day 8: Ps.17; Jn.8.31-2
Day 9: Ps.20; Jn.14.15-7
Day 10: Ps.30.1-5; Jn.10.7,9,10,14-5
Day 11: Ps.30.6-12; Jn.16.20-1
Day 12: Ps.38; Jn.9.3-5
Day 13: Ps.41; Jn.13.34-5
Day 14: Ps.48; Jn.14.12-4
Day 15: Ps.52; Lk.7.38,47
Day 16: Ps.55; Jn.16.33
Day 17: Ps.59; Jn.8.12
Day 18: Ps.62; Jn.12.44-8
Day 19: Ps.63; Jn.16.12-5
Day 20: Ps.84; Jn.15.4-5
Day 21: Ps.93; Jn.17.3-5
Day 22: Ps.96; Jn.1.43,45-7
Day 23: Ps.98; Jn.18.36-7
Day 24: Ps.106; Jn.20.21-3
Day 25: Ps.107.23-32; Jn.14.6-7
Day 26: Ps.108; Lk.10.41-2
Day 27: Ps.111; Lk.12.6-7
Day 28: Ps.115; Lk.13.18-21
Day 29: Ps.122; Jn.6.67-9
Day 30: Ps.131;133; Jn.17.20-1
Day 31: Ps.137; Mt.13.44-6

Prayers: The first prayer is based on a collect in the Alternative Service Book. The source of the second I have not been able to trace, but wish to acknowledge with thanks. The third and fourth prayers are by St Teresa of Avila. The fifth prayer is derived from a comment on the function of poetry by Pablo Neruda. The last prayer is part of St. Patrick's Breastplate, tr. Mrs. C.F.Alexander (NEH159).

ACKNOWLEDGMENTS
With thanks for permission to reprint copyright material:

Ms M.J.Huntspil, Estate of J.B.Peacey, for the hymn, *For Mary, Mother of the Lord* by J.B.Peacey.

The Friends of York Minster for the prayer for Easter by Eric Milner-White from *My God, my Glory*, SPCK, 1967, p.58.

Hymns Ancient and Modern Ltd. for the hymn, *Good Christian men rejoice and sing*, by C.A.Alington.

The Joint Liturgical Group for the canticle, *Glory and honour*, from *The Daily Office*, SPCK, 1978.

The Central Board of Finance of the Church of England, for the Easter Preface from the Alternative Service Book, H&S, 1980.

The SCM Press Ltd. for the second prayer on p.122, based on words of J.V.Taylor, *The Primal Vision*, SCM 1963.